NORTH CAROLINA
SHARK
ATTACKS

NORTH CAROLINA
SHARK ATTACKS

A HISTORY

JOHN HAIRR

THE
History
PRESS

Published by The History Press
Charleston, SC
www.historypress.com

All photographs by the author unless otherwise noted.

First published 2023

Manufactured in the United States

ISBN 9781467153959

Library of Congress Control Number: 2022950075

CONTENTS

INTRODUCTION

I have been chronicling man's interactions with marine life along the southeastern United States for many years and was fortunate, on several occasions, to have an opportunity to discuss marine megafauna with Dr. Frank Schwartz of the University of North Carolina's Institute of Marine Sciences in Morehead City. There, if one timed it right, a person could drop by his lab and not only hear about his recent adventures on the seas but also see what specimens and other tangible items had been brought back from the ocean. These were mainly sharks and other related items, but on occasion, he might show a jar full of some mysterious deep-sea animal brought in by a local fisherman to see if Dr. Schwartz could help figure out what exactly the lucky fisherman had brought back from the deep. Dr. Schwartz's long and voluminous publication record, especially in the *Journal of the Elisha Mitchel Scientific Society*, stands as a testimony to his wide and varied interest in the natural history of his adopted state of North Carolina. Dr. Schwartz was a true gentleman and scholar who freely shared his knowledge of what he found in the waters off North Carolina, especially the elasmobranch fauna about which he was so passionate.

In the past, editors of several popular magazines have asked me to write articles regarding shark attacks, especially off North Carolina, but I declined, concentrating previous works on the sharks themselves. Over the years, while researching various maritime-related projects, I amassed quite a collection of accounts of people's misadventures with sharks off the coast of the southeastern United States, forwarding them when appropriate to the folks at the International Shark Attack File, who keep an official tally of such incidents. But over the past decade, there has been much misinformation about sharks, especially the early history of people's interactions with sharks—so much so that I feel it is appropriate to preserve this important piece of maritime history by completing this volume dedicated to shark attacks off North Carolina for The History Press. Some might be disappointed in not finding within the pages of this book any official police evidence photographs of bloody, mangled limbs, ripped torsos, decapitated bodies and the like. But what they will find is as accurate a chronicle as possible of the history of shark attacks off North Carolina as can be pieced together from very limited source material.

You also will not find any photographs of recent shark attack victims themselves. No matter how many years may have passed since an incident occurred, emotional scars may remain with survivors or extended family members that need not be revisited via photographic means.

Dr. Schwartz was a pioneer in the study of the life history of sharks and rays found off the coast of North Carolina and adjacent waters. In the process of studying the biology of these animals, he drudged up many accounts of the negative interactions between sharks and humans. Thus, almost reluctantly, he became an expert on the study of shark attacks off our coast. With the media frenzy unleashed by the *Jaws* movies back in the 1970s, he became the go-to guy for newspaper editors trying to flesh out their otherwise dry stories copied straight from the police blotter chronicling mayhem along the beach. He had to walk a fine line between freely sharing the knowledge he had gathered as a member of a public university at the taxpayers' expense with the media sensationalizing what he found and causing a panic.

The evolution of Dr. Schwartz's knowledge of shark attacks off North Carolina can be seen in his first booklet chronicling the elasmobranch fauna of the state, *Sharks of North Carolina and Adjacent Waters*, which was cowritten with his colleague at the University of North Carolina's Institute of Marine Sciences George H. Burgess in 1975. They devote only a single paragraph to the state's shark attacks, pointing out that Jere Fountain and Rupert Wade's attacks were the only two that could be authenticated from North Carolina. In their book, they observed, "Both Fountain and Wade succumbed to their wounds. Surprisingly, no other authentic attacks, other than those attributed to bluefish or barracudas, have occurred despite the increased use of the seashore areas by thousands of people between March and November."

Over two decades after his initial publications on the subject, Schwartz, in 2003, was able to document twenty-three shark attacks dating back to 1870, of which seven were fatal. "Most were caused by bull sharks, although three of the five attacks in 2000 were caused by blacktip sharks." Based on several factors, Schwartz came up with the following conclusions: "Twenty of the recorded attacks occurred in the afternoon during ebbing tides, regardless of whether the attack took place in the ocean or in Pamlico Sound." He also includes a handy chart he drew showing phases of the moon and meteorological conditions—if known—at the time of the respective attack.

Burgess later became a curator of the International Shark Attack File after its archives were transferred to the Florida Museum of Natural History at the University of Florida in Gainesville in 1988. The material they gathered started in the 1950s with the Office of Naval Research's efforts to create a comprehensive archive of all known shark attacks. The main reasons behind its creation were safety related, as it was hoped that studying such attacks might help researchers find ways to avoid them in the future.

Shark attacks can basically be divided into two categories: provoked and unprovoked. Provoked incidents include those that are caused by the shark reacting to an interaction with a human, such as a fisherman trying to free a shark from a hook or line. Another would be when a shark is following a blood trail or chum left behind to draw in the sharks for both fishermen and tourists. Many of Russell Coles's shark attacks mentioned later in this book are clearly provoked incidents. Unprovoked attacks occur when a shark launches an attack without human stimulation. This includes surprise attacks, such as when a shark appears on the scene from out of the blue and takes a bite out of its victim. A sort of gray area would be when a shark bites its victim but initiates the attack as a bit of mistaken identity, like biting a surfer because they and their board look much like a turtle or other item on which the shark regularly feeds when viewed from the depths below. Bull sharks, for instance, are known to bite and release many of their victims, testing to see if their prey is something worth investing the effort to kill and consume.

While we still do not know the exact reasons an individual shark is compelled to act in any particular attack, one can reason that some incidents are based simply on the fact that the shark was doing what predators do—hunting for prey. Hunger can be quite a motivator, especially for carnivorous animals. Sometimes, humans cavorting about in the surf will actually get in the way of a shark and the smaller fish on which it feeds, and thus, a shark can actually bite a person while feeding on the smaller fish. That's why it is generally a good rule of thumb not to swim in waters on occasions when large schools of bait fish are jumping above the surface of the sea, as they are most likely being chased by larger fish from below, including sharks.

A study of shark attack data compiled over the last half of the twentieth century by researchers with the International Shark Attack File shows that most unprovoked attacks happen in nearshore waters and can be grouped into three main categories. Hit and run attacks are when a shark bites a person as it is just passing through a given area. Bump and bite attacks usually occur in deeper waters and tend to indicate the shark has developed more of an interest in its potential victim, sizing them up while often circling or bumping into the potential prey to see if what has piqued its interest is worth the effort needed to obtain a meal. The final category are sneak attacks, or instances in which sharks attack without warning. Most sneak attacks result in serious injury or even death. A study of the historical record shows that all three of these types of shark attacks have occurred in North Carolina waters.

Though Schwartz and Burgess helped shed light on more recent shark attacks, an often-overlooked scholar of these incidents in the Carolinas was E. Milby Burton, a director of the Charleston Museum, who became curious in the 1930s about why there were so few authentic shark attack records from the coast of the southeastern United States. He set out to discover if there were any incidents along the Carolina coast that had gone unrecorded. By examining hospital records and interviewing several individuals, he chronicled seven incidents that were unequivocally shark attacks that had occurred along the coast nearby between 1907 and 1933. He heard rumours of several others but was unable to authenticate the attacks.

Burton, in 1935, noted some of the difficulties he encountered in his research. "Invariably, when an attack of this kind occurs, everyone immediately concludes 'barracuda.' In many respects, this is quite understandable, as the psychological effect would be extremely bad and no one would frequent the bathing beaches.…The great barracuda (*Sphyreana barracuda*) is apparently very rare in and around Charleston." Why Burton and his contemporaries found the idea of being attacked by a barracuda over a shark more plausible is unclear. Perhaps they reasoned that since a barracuda is much smaller than the larger shark species that inhabit our coast, it is unlikely a person could be eaten and completely consumed by a barracuda, and thus, a human stands a better chance of walking away from a run-in with a barracuda.

There have been numerous shark attacks documented along the Carolina coast since Burton conducted his ground-breaking research. Many of the

Palmetto State attacks he missed will be covered in a future volume. Shark attacks have occurred in all of the North Carolina counties bordering the Atlantic Ocean, from Currituck County in the north to Brunswick County in the south. The majority of cases come from the waters of New Hanover County, while Carteret County is home to the most shark fatalities.

This project builds on these earlier works and is an effort to document encounters between people and sharks in North Carolina waters. Most of these attacks, especially those in the more distant past, are nearly forgotten and poorly understood today. It is hoped that by providing basic information about these events, researchers will benefit from new insights into the nature of these apex predators and their interactions with people. There are entries for every known fatal shark attack listed, as well as other significant attacks on both people and watercraft. Much of the data comes from accounts published in the popular media, especially newspaper or magazine accounts gathered over the years from a variety of publications, each of which is listed in the bibliography.

1

PROJECT OVERVIEW

The most dangerous part of a visit to the beaches of North Carolina in the early twenty-first century is, without question, the drive down on the overcrowded highways, with millions of people flocking to the state's beaches from all over the world in the summer, looking for fun in the sun. If a person survives the harrowing trip, other hazards, such being struck by lightning, drowned, stung by a jellyfish, barbed by a stingray or caught in a rip current and whisked away into the briny deep beyond the range of help, pose real threats to a person's well-being. All of these calamities are much more likely to end one's vacation in coastal North Carolina than an encounter with a shark.

Sharks are just one of the many risks tourist promoters often overlook in their zeal to entice folk to head down to splash about in these "idyllic" seas or soak up some rays. But in reality, the shores of North Carolina are much more dangerous than a jaunt to a New England pond, so one should always factor that into their travel plans before setting off for the sunny South. Unfortunately, many people have flocked to the fragile barrier islands that make up the Outer Banks, bringing some of their overpopulation problems with them—mainly pollution. One of the most recent examples was an advisory posted by the National Park Service for beachgoers to be sure to wear hard-soled shoes if venturing onto the beach, as many of the condos that have been unwisely built there, precariously close to the shore on the ever-shifting sands of the Outer Banks, are washing into the sea, thus depositing all of those materials real estate developers claimed were impervious to Mother Nature into the ocean. There, nails, glass, broken wood and other dangerous items wait to skewer or gash a hunk of flesh from one's unguarded feet.

Inhabitants of the northern Outer Banks have gone to great lengths to earn a living from their sometimes bleak and unproductive land. Long before they began coaxing northern tourists to their resort settlement at Nag's Head, wily Bankers tied lanterns around the necks of mules and set them loose on the high dunes, like Jockey's Ridge, during cloudy or foggy weather, thus tricking unwary mariners into believing they had passed beyond the dangers of Cape Hatteras. Instead, after they turned west, they heard the roar of the breakers too late to correct the error and found themselves wrecked on a lonely stretch of sand, their vessel destroyed by the savage pounding of the sea and their crew often devoured by sharks.

In the not-too-distant past, before air conditioning allowed people to insulate themselves from their natural environment, coastal North Carolina and the rest of the southeastern United States was a harsh place, inhabited by hardy people. The deadliest creatures were not the large marine animals, like sharks or killer whales, but tiny insects, namely flies of the family Culicidae commonly called mosquitoes. We will never know just how many of our ancestors died due to mosquito-borne illnesses, such as yellow fever and malaria. Most of the mosquito-borne illnesses were knocked out in coastal communities of North Carolina thanks to an aggressive use of insecticides and draining low-lying swampy areas where possible. But illnesses such as encephalitis and West Nile virus are proving resilient.

The reason for mentioning these insects is simple: to add a bit of perspective to my account of these shark attacks. For example, more people died from the yellow fever outbreak in Wilmington in the summer of 1861 than during all of North Carolina's documented shark attacks since the days when John White lost Sir Walter Raleigh's colony at Roanoke Island over five centuries ago. However, if we allow that half of the people who died over the centuries in the infamous "Graveyard of the Atlantic" were devoured by sharks, that sheds a new light on the equation, helping us understand why mariners viewed these animals lurking beneath the waters with such trepidation.

The true number of shark attacks that have occurred in the waters of North Carolina is far higher than the number officially recorded. There are a couple of reasons for this. One is the likelihood that several incidents went unrecorded because of the remote nature of the region, as television news crews have not always stalked the shores of our state, ready to pounce on some

Nag's Head has long been popular with tourists, as evidenced by this illustration, which graced the pages of *Harper's Weekly* in 1857. Though there were many rumors of shark attacks throughout the nineteenth century, the earliest documented shark-related fatality here was the death of Frank Hines in August 1882.

poor soul to broadcast their misfortune around the world in nanoseconds, even before the arrival of emergency medical teams.

People did not usually call the police when they were nipped by a shark—at least not North Carolinians visiting the beaches into the 1970s—unless the wounds were serious enough to need the attention of a physician or the attack resulted in a fatality. So, prior to the mid-twentieth century, the chances of someone actually being on hand to document such an incident required an unlikely combination of timing a correspondent's visit to the shore with an actual attack worthy of being written about.

Perhaps the main reasons there are so few authenticated reports of shark attacks off the Carolina coast is that many incidents of more serious shark attacks were quickly downplayed by those responsible for promoting the region. Attacks were often called drownings, even in cases where witnesses saw the victim struggling with some sort of animal in bloodstained water. The official report would say that the person must have drowned, and the shark in question was just cleaning up the dead carrion. This answer seemed plausible to folks with a cursory knowledge of the sea's creatures, because many shark species do in fact act as scavengers, showing up like other denizens of the deep to feast on a welcome meal. Such reasoning also may have been more comforting to those who had to make their way into the water as fishermen, especially those who spent lots of time wading in the salty waters of the North Carolina coast, tending fishing nets.

Another term has been offered up in the early days of the twenty-first century in an effort to downplay the danger posed by sharks in the world's oceans: shark accidents. Some have even argued that humans are clearly at fault in all such "accidents," since we are trespassing in the watery realm where we do not belong. Such musings may seem harmless or even a bit comical at first, but they unfortunately take sharks and humans out of their respective roles as apex predators in the ocean and turn sharks into some sort of benign cartoon characters, swimming about in their oceanic realm and never harming anyone unless forced into defending themselves as a last resort. It also demonstrates a deep misunderstanding of man's long history of dealing with large animals like sharks, with which man has struggled across the ages.

Millions of years of evolution have developed the lethal killing machines we commonly refer to as sharks. The planet's elasmobranchs should be studied as closely as possible so we can learn more about the important part they play in the natural world. Anyone who has given these creatures more than a cursory study realizes they are lethal predators capable of exploiting their respective niche in the marine ecosystem.

Sharks and humans have been interacting for millennia, and we can only wonder what went through the minds of our ancient forebears as they made their initial steps along the edge of the salty seas by floating on bundles of sticks or inflated animal skins to venture offshore, attempting to hunt and fish in this mysterious watery world. They often watched in horror as many of their kinsmen were devoured by the denizens of the deep, including sharks. Whether motivated by our innate sense of curiosity, desperation in the face of starvation or perhaps a combination of all, these early people mastered the rudiments of hunting from small craft such as canoes and kayaks. Over time, people developed an innate hatred for sharks—on one hand respecting them as a worthy adversary but, in most cases, seeing them as competitors for fish and small marine mammals. Thus, before people had the leisure to study sharks in a scientific fashion, they saw them not only as a natural resource to be exploited but also as a fierce competitor that stole food from their fishing lines or nets. The larger species of sharks were more than just a nuisance, however, as most

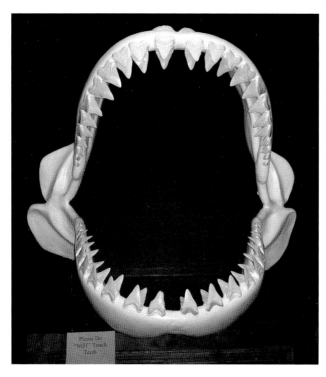

Left: Megalodon jaw.

Below: The beaches of Brunswick County have been the scene of several shark attacks over the years.

had the frightening ability to strike without warning and kill one of their companions in an instant.

At some point during the twentieth century, however, the balance in the struggle between man and his fellow predators shifted decidedly in favour of the humans. This was due in no small part to man's great technological advances, which led to an over-exploitation of virtually all of the world's finite resources, including those in the oceanic realm. Many of the ramifications of this over-industrialisation are now coming home— even here in North Carolina, where fishermen a century ago were still able to rely on local stocks of fish to feed their communities, but today, there are clearly nowhere near the number of fish available to feed the multitudes of people now living along the North Carolina coast without bringing in fish from far afield.

2

WORLD'S LARGEST AND DEADLIEST SHARKS CALL NORTH CAROLINA HOME

People today have no concept of just how extensive the shark population here off North Carolina was prior to the nineteenth century. Such a bountiful supply of raw material drew commercial shark fishermen, who set up industrialized operations here, especially along the coast of Carteret County. Sharks were caught and taken not necessarily for the meat or fins but mainly for the skins. As a matter of fact, most of the meat from these early shark operations was thought to be undesirable, and the by-product ended up being ground up into fertilizer.

The Ocean Leather Corporation built a factory in Morehead City, near where the North Carolina Marine Fisheries Complex stands today, almost on the very spot where Dr. Schwartz's office at the University of North Carolina's Institute of Marine Sciences was located. Schwartz and Burgess, in 1975, described the plant that was built in 1919 along the southern shore of Bogue Sound:

> The operation was directed by E. Young. Originally, a pier was built extending out into deep water. A skinning and dissecting platform was constructed on the pier to shield the sharks and their by-products from the hot sun. A curing, storage, and by-product building was also completed. Later, a shark liver oil plant was established, complete with a narrow-gauge railroad from the end of the pier to the building and processing facilities.

Captain Thomas Young, in his book *Shadows in the Sea: The Sharks, Skates and Rays*, gives a detailed account of the Ocean Leather Corporation's Morehead City operation, complete with a shark skinning diagram.

One of the main arguments behind targeting sharks in such a fashion was to relieve the pressure on some of the more desirable food fish upon which both humans and sharks relied. Another reason was to develop a new source of oil, thus taking some of the pressure off whales and other marine mammals. As Frederick J. Haskin (1918) pointed out, "This new shark business is to serve a quadruple use. It is to add to our food supply, our oil supply, our leather supply, and to conserve other food fishes by reducing the numbers of the sharks—for all sharks are voracious beasts of prey."

We are fortunate that during this period of transition in the ecological balance, scientists such as Russell Coles, Lewis Radcliffe, H.M. Smith, Henry Yarrow, E.W. Gudger, H.H. Brimley and his brother C.S. Brimley began studying the remarkable marine fauna they found here along the coast. Both shark fishermen and the naturalists drawn to the area were valuable links in helping develop a systematic nomenclature for the shark species found in our waters. They helped the local folks identify the sharks they had been dealing with for generations, assisting with the transition from using outdated common names for sharks, such as shovel heads, balance heads or sand sharks.

These commercial shark operations kept no records of the number of employees who were killed or maimed while landing their catch or processing the fish ashore. They no doubt saw these provoked attacks as occupational hazards, not worthy of complaint nor worth the effort of keeping a permanent record. Evidence that this way of thinking survived well into the twentieth century is given by shark fishermen who were bitten on their feet and legs after landing several particularly aggressive blue sharks just offshore in 1963. Their attacks would have gone unnoticed had a researcher not been on board the moment they occurred (Schwartz, 1985).

Few remember that people along the southern Outer Banks have been dealing with large sharks, particularly great whites, for many years. The honor of the first documented landing of a great white shark along the North Carolina coast belongs to a group of whalers. Captain Lorenzo Willis and his crew of shore-based whalers inadvertently harpooned the memorable fish in early May 1888 in Carteret County, off Shackleford Banks, just a short distance from the Cape Lookout Lighthouse.

The Willis family of Carteret County has a long tradition of making their living from the seas along the southern Outer Banks of North Carolina.

The bull shark is one of the most dangerous species of sharks found in the nearshore waters of North Carolina. In addition to frequenting large shallow estuarian waters, such as Pamlico and Albemarle Sounds, these sharks also lurk upstream in the state's freshwater rivers, including the Waccamaw, Neuse, Chowan and Cape Fear Rivers.

In days gone by, this family was renowned for producing some of the most expert fishermen and whalers in the region. It should come as no surprise that a member of this family who spent so much of their time on the water should be involved in what was so far the earliest known account of the capture of a great white shark along the North Carolina coast.

People who lived along the barrier islands from Bear Island in Onslow County up the Outer Banks to Cape Hatteras maintained a whale "fishery" throughout the eighteenth and nineteenth centuries. This came to an end during the early years of the twentieth century thanks to the decimation of the cetaceans on which they relied (mainly right whales due primarily to overhunting elsewhere in its range). To supplement their farming or fishing income—and to get some hard currency—many hardy souls along this stretch of coast often put to sea in pursuit of whales. Unlike the New England brand of pelagic whaling, the whaling in North Carolina was shore-based. Lookouts were posted along the high dunes to scan the horizon for whales. When one was spotted, a signal was given, and crews of men would converge on the scene to put out to sea in pursuit of the whales.

The whalers put to sea in whaleboats propelled by oars. They rowed on the open ocean, sometimes for many miles, until they caught up with the whale, and then the harpooner let fly with his harpoons. If all went well, they eventually closed with their prey, killing it with blows from specially designed lances. The whale's carcass was then towed back to shore, where the animal

A shore-based whaling crew operating off Shackleford Banks. *A North Carolina Department of Agriculture image.*

was processed for oil, bone and any other commodity the inhabitants could get from their prize.

Captain Willis's group was composed of men who lived along the Shackleford Banks, not far from Diamond City. On a cool morning in May 1888, Captain Willis and his crew were working in the waters just west of Cape Lookout. Whether they had been called out in pursuit of a whale that got away or were just cruising about practicing their skills is unknown. As they worked their way along the coast, they came to a landmark known as Wreck Point, the tip of the sandy spit that stretches west from Cape Lookout back toward Shackleford Banks. The waters contained between Wreck Point and the Shackleford Banks are called Lookout Bight, or simply the Bight. A short distance off Wreck Point, one of the crewmen spotted a large animal swimming near the surface of the water. The experienced crew manoeuvred their whaleboat into position, and the harpooner let fly his weapon. The throw struck its mark.

We can only imagine what surprise Captain Willis and his men experienced when they realized their target was no mere whale, the prey they normally fought. Instead, an enormous shark with a mouth full of razor-sharp teeth jumped clear out of the water. A fierce struggle between man and fish ensued. Willis and his crew battled this shark for more than two hours. They were fortunate that the animal was in relatively shallow water and did not have the opportunity to dive deeper than their length of rope. We don't know exactly how he did it, but the harpooner was finally able to kill the huge fish after a long, desperate fight.

The shark was secured to their whaleboat and towed ashore, where Captain Willis and his men hoped to learn more about their strange catch. They found it to be eighteen feet long and eight feet wide across its pectorals. They claimed the shark weighed two tons, but whether this was an accurate measurement or an educated guess is unknown.

After measuring the shark, the whalers decided to dissect its body. Inside the shark's stomach, they found the remains of six sharks, the smallest of which measured six feet long. "His mouth was large enough to roll a kerosene barrel into with room to spare," wrote an unnamed correspondent for the newspaper in the nearby town of Beaufort in 1888. "He had three rows of teeth, one inch wide and two inches long. Our oldest fisherman pronounced him to be the largest ever killed on our coast."

Fishermen along the North Carolina coast in those days did not differentiate sharks by species the way we do today. Instead, they grouped them in such categories as "hammerheads" or "maneaters." This was a couple of decades before the more systematic naming of sharks took hold, so sharks were not broken down into the various orders and species with which we are now familiar. It is doubtful that Captain Willis or any of his men on the beach that day back in 1888 realized the significance of their catch or ever knew the true identity of the shark they hauled in.

Although Captain Willis never described the exact species of shark they caught, it is possible to conclude that it was a great white thanks to a number of factors. There are not many species of sharks cruising North Carolina waters large enough to have been the one caught by Captain Willis. About half a dozen fit the bill, including tiger sharks, great white sharks, Greenland sharks, cow sharks, whale sharks and basking sharks. The latter three species can be ruled out based on what the fishermen found inside the shark after they cut it open on the beach. Whale sharks and basking sharks feed on plankton and krill. Neither of these species consume large fish like the six sharks in excess of six feet long that were found inside Captain Willis's shark.

Cow sharks are among the largest sharks in the ocean. Some have been observed that measured over twenty-five feet long. Cow sharks do indeed consume large fish, including sharks. Cow sharks are occasionally found in nearshore waters. A relatively famous specimen was found in the wee hours of the morning of March 14, 1886, by a surfman. He was patrolling

Whale sharks like this one in the Georgia Aquarium are found along the North Carolina coast, as well as in the Cape Fear River. These large sharks are not considered dangerous to people.

the lonely shores of the northern Outer Banks of North Carolina when he noticed a large object in the surf. Unknown to him, he had stumbled upon the remains of an infrequent visitor to the North Carolina coast.

What he found was a cow shark, *Hexanchus griseus*. These sharks are also widely known as bluntnose sixgill sharks, as they sport six gill openings on each side of their body. These brownish-colored sharks are often found in water over six thousand feet deep but are known to come close to the shore and surface on occasion. These rare sharks are seldom seen off the North Carolina coast, with only five specimens besides this one being observed off both North and South Carolina between 1886 and 2000.

When the surfman and his mates back at the Currituck Inlet Life Saving Station examined their mysterious fish, they noticed the creature's unusual teeth. What they may not have discerned was the shark's "third eye," a pale patch of skin on the top of a cow shark's head. Scientists today are unsure of the exact function of this "organ." Some theories maintain that since these sharks live so much of their lives in the abyssal depths, the light-sensitive tissue is used to help them stay oriented properly with the ocean's surface.

Correspondence still preserved in the records of the Smithsonian Institution give us several details about how the remains of this rare shark

Teeth from a Currituck cow shark. *Photograph by Sandra Raredon of the Division of Marine Fisheries, NMNH, Smithsonian Institution.*

were saved for further study. Keeper D.M. Etheridge was intrigued and baffled by the unusual fish that had washed ashore near the Currituck Inlet station. He wisely decided to contact the U.S. National Museum to see if it would be interested in this odd find. That afternoon, he dispatched a telegram that read, "Awash. Fish unknown specimen was sent ashore three am ten feet long twenty-one inches deep fourteen inches wide peculiar teeth."

Apparently, the message piqued the interest of the folks at the museum in Washington, D.C., and they relayed their interest back to Etheridge. On March 16, 1886, he had the remains of his unusual fish crated up and placed aboard the steamer *Bonito*, bound for the nation's capital. The steamer made the journey in two days, and the shark's remains became part of the U.S. National Museum's collection on March 18, 1886. Once in Washington, the cow shark was measured and carefully studied. T.H. Bean catalogued the specimen and officially identified the remains as *Hexanchus griseus*. Next, a plaster cast was made and placed on exhibit in the museum.

The cow shark from Currituck Inlet remained on display for many years at what is now known as the Smithsonian Institution Museum of Natural History. Time, however, was not kind to the plaster casts that were utilized by museums throughout the world in those days. All that remains of the only cow shark ever found on the shores of North Carolina are pieces from its jaws and teeth. Fortunately, the remains of the shark from Currituck are still being preserved at the Smithsonian, as an examination of the teeth show they do not match descriptions of the shark's teeth from Willis's shark harpooned off Cape Lookout in 1888.

One of the most enigmatic fish in the sea, Greenland sharks, *Somniosus microcephalus*, are another of the large species of sharks found off North Carolina. Unlike most shark species, they live predominantly in the cold waters of the polar and subpolar regions of the Arctic. They are found at great depths, in excess of a mile below the ocean's surface. When mature, these sometimes-lethargic sharks average approximately fifteen feet in length. Sometimes, they may grow as large as twenty-four feet long and weigh over a ton. They can assume a variety of colors, including gray,

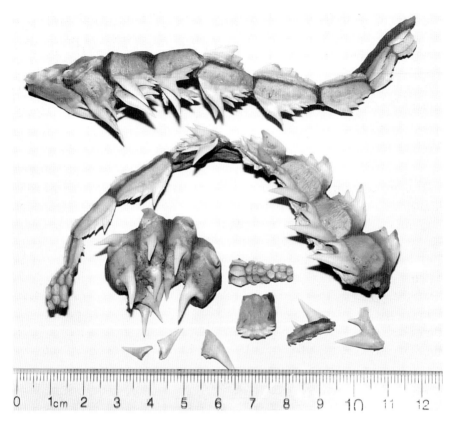

Fragments of a jaw and teeth are all that remain of the cow shark that was stranded at Currituck Inlet in 1886. *Photograph by Sandra Raredon of the Division of Marine Fisheries, NMNH, Smithsonian Institution.*

brown, black and even purple. Some have white spots on their sides, while others have dark bands. Studies done in recent years show that they can live for more than a century.

One characteristic Greenland sharks do share with many other shark species is that they are not very discerning about what they eat. The Greenland shark's diet consists mainly of fish, but they will also eat hapless marine mammals if the opportunity presents itself. Bright (2000) noted that in the cold winter months, these sharks will eat just about anything that comes along, and he pointed out that "parts of a horse, an entire reindeer (minus horns), and a seaman's leg, complete with sea boot, have been found in the stomach."

For centuries, people inhabiting the Arctic regions of America and Europe caught Greenland sharks and ate them. The Icelandic delicacy

Greenland shark. *Photograph by Heather Bowlby, Canadian Atlantic Shark Research Lab, Fisheries Canada.*

hakarl, made from fermented Greenland shark, is perhaps the most well-known example of this consumption. They are notoriously easy to catch and put up little fight when hooked. Some Inuit are reported to have used blocks of wood for bait.

Though the Greenland shark may be easy to bring in, preparing the catch is a different story. Due to a chemical in the shark's flesh, thought to be trimethylamine, the meat of these sharks is toxic if eaten raw. Those familiar with the preparation of this fish claim that it has to be boiled three times before it is fit for human consumption. Furthermore, if a dog drinks the water in which the fish is boiled, it will become terribly sick and may even die.

When discussing the various species of marine animals that were poisonous for humans to consume, Dr. Bruce Halstead (1959) pointed out that most illnesses were caused by sharks encountered in the tropics—with the exception of the Greenland shark. He noted, "Most illnesses have been caused by tropical species, and the most severe poisonings have resulted from eating the livers of tropical sharks. However, the flesh of the Greenland shark, *Somniosus microcephalus*, Bloch and Schneider, which inhabits Arctic waters, has been observed to cause intoxication in both humans and sled dogs. The chemical nature of these poisons is not known."

There are no records of Greenland sharks becoming stranded along the beaches of North Carolina. Only two specimens have been observed in the waters offshore this far south. Schwartz (2003) reported that one was taken off Cape Hatteras in the 1980s: "A 6.4-meter-long Greenland shark (*Somniosus microcephalus*), a northern species that usually inhabits cold water, was captured near Cape Hatteras in 703-meter waters."

The southernmost sighting of a Greenland shark in the waters of the western Atlantic Ocean was made off the coast of South Carolina/Georgia in 1990. Charles Herdendorf and several members of the Columbus America Discovery Group on board the RV *Arctic Discovery* saw a large animal

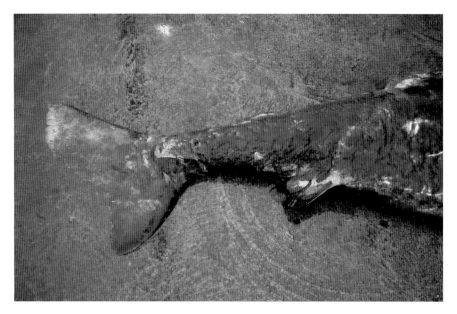

A close-up look at the tail of a Greenland shark. *Photograph by Heather Bowlby, Canadian Atlantic Shark Research Lab, Fisheries Canada.*

pass by the lens of their remote-controlled video camera on the morning of September 1, 1990. This camera was attached to an unmanned research submersible called *Nemo* that was nearly 7,500 feet deep on the bottom of the Atlantic Ocean at a feature known as the Blake Ridge, approximately 150 miles east of the mouth of the Savannah River, which forms the boundary between South Carolina and Georgia. They were looking for artifacts relating to the SS *Central America*, a steamship that went down in a hurricane in September 1857. The wreck claimed the lives of over four hundred people, and the ship was reputed to be carrying millions of dollars' worth of gold.

Curious to see what kind of marine life they would attract at such depths, the researchers placed an assortment of baits and fish carcasses near the wreck site. They observed several parasitic eels and other fish feeding off their bait and then noticed the large shark just as their submersible was returning to the surface. What the investigators saw that night was later identified as a Greenland shark measuring nearly twenty feet long. Herdendorf and Berra noted, "We estimated its length by comparing the shark's image with an imprint of when *Nemo* had recently landed on the ocean floor. The shark appeared just as *Nemo* was lifting off, brushed against one of the camera booms and then moved toward the pile of fish carcasses."

When commenting on the importance of this sighting, Herdendorf and Berra pointed out, "The depth is 1,000 meters deeper than the maximum reported depth for the species. The Savannah location is 440 kilometers farther south than the previously known North Carolina records for the Greenland shark."

Greenland sharks have long been targeted by the inhabitants of the Arctic on both sides of the Atlantic as a source of both food and oil. One nineteenth-century naturalist who observed Greenland sharks was Sir William Dawson. Dawson (1891) examined many of the fish specimens that were captured at Little Metis Island near the mouth of the St. Lawrence River off the coast of Quebec, including several Greenland sharks. He noted that halibut fishermen occasionally hooked specimens of this particular species of shark as a bycatch for their targeted species. "Five or six specimens, some ten feet in length, were thus taken and towed ashore last summer. They are not valued for food, but the liver yields a considerable quantity of oils, and the skin is used as a rasp for dressing wood."

Bigelow and Schroeder (1953) believed these sharks to be "entirely inoffensive to man" and noted further, "Tales to the effect that it attacks Greenlanders in their kayaks are apparently mythical, and Dr. Porsild, director of the Biological Station at Disko, said that the Eskimos do not fear it as they do the killer whale; nor is there any authentic instance on record of a shark attacking a human in Iceland."

Bigelow's and Schroeder's contention that Greenland sharks were relatively harmless to humans was corroborated by personal observations of pelagic whalers operating in the Arctic waters. An anonymous newspaper account from 1902 states:

> *The Greenland shark is well known as a foe to whalers. It will follow a dead whale to the ship and show no fear of the men while they are engaged in cutting up the prey, biting out lumps from it as big as a man's head. Sometimes it happens that a man will fall off the slippery side of the whale close by the shark, but the latter never attacks him, being intent upon gorging itself with the flesh of the cetacean. The most severe wounds from thrusts of the whalers' knives will not persuade it to desist. This species of shark is often partly or wholly blinded by a parasitic worm three inches long which fastens itself at the corner of the eye and lives on its fluids.*

In the days when the pelagic whaling industry was in full swing, Greenland sharks would often follow whaling ships back to their home ports in New

England, driven mad with hunger for the putrid remains of the dead whales. Greenland sharks were one of the species of sharks menacing pelagic whalers working offshore in the Hatteras Grounds off the Outer Banks. It is not unreasonable to contend that these large sharks followed the cetacean carcasses to inshore waters along the North Carolina coast in much the same fashion that they did in northern waters. The ravenous sharks may even have been attracted to the whale carcasses left behind by the shore-based whalers off Cape Lookout. But we can rule out this species of shark as the one harpooned by Willis and his crew thanks to descriptions of the shark's teeth, which were clearly not from a Greenland shark.

Tiger sharks consume large fish and just about anything else they can get their mouths on. There are tiger sharks eighteen feet in length prowling along the North Carolina coast, but they are not known to reach such large dimensions as eight feet across the pectorals, nor do they weigh two tons. According to the International Game Fish Association, the largest tiger shark ever taken on a rod and reel was caught by Walter Maxwell near the North Carolina–South Carolina border in 1964; it measured over thirteen feet long and weighed 1,780 pounds, an IGFA all-tackle world record.

The description of Willis's shark's teeth points to the fact that this was not a tiger shark. Captain Willis's shark was described as having "three rows of teeth an inch wide and two inches long." A tiger shark has teeth that are curved, much like the teeth on the blade of a circular saw—they are not triangular. Meanwhile, great whites have triangular-shaped teeth of the size and dimensions described.

Aside from the description of the shark itself, it is important to take into account local weather conditions at the time. The weather in early May 1888 was described as being unusually cold, with strong winds out of the north—not the conditions that would normally appeal to tiger sharks, which prefer warmer conditions.

From the descriptions of the shark that were penned at the time by the unnamed correspondent who saw the shark and spoke with its captors, we can conclude that Captain Willis and his men off the Shackleford Banks caught a great white, a large species of shark with triangular teeth that eats other large sharks, enjoys cooler waters and frequents the southern Outer Banks. Through the years, there have been several encounters with great white sharks along the North Carolina coast, from Currituck south to the Cape Fear. Though new accounts are surfacing as we learn more about the ocean, Captain Willis's shark remains the earliest documented great white taken in the waters off North Carolina.

A tiger shark caught off the pier at Nag's Head. *An Aycock Brown photograph, courtesy of the Outer Banks History Center.*

According to Dr. Schwartz's detailed records, the largest great white taken along the North Carolina coast in recent years was caught approximately twenty miles south of Beaufort Inlet in April 1986 by some longline fishermen out of Morehead City. This shark measured fifteen feet, nine inches long and weighed 2,143.26 pounds. Perhaps the most memorable great white

Left: A great white shark caught in 1984 off the North Carolina coast. *Photograph courtesy of North Carolina Archives and History.*

Opposite: A juvenile great white shark caught by Russell Coles in 1918. *Photograph courtesy of the National Marine Fisheries Service.*

taken in these waters during the second half of the twentieth century was one taken by Captain Lloyd Davidson, Jon Dodrill and Sylvester Karasinski aboard the shark fishing boat *Alligator* on September 25, 1984. That shark, a female that measured fifteen feet, six inches long and weighed 2,080 pounds, drew crowds of curious onlookers to the Morehead City waterfront. It even made an appearance at the North Carolina State Fair in Raleigh. Today, a mount of the shark peers down at visitors from a wall near the entrance to the North Carolina Maritime Museum at Beaufort.

One of the largest great white sharks officially chronicled anywhere in the world was measured in North Carolina waters off Carteret County, just offshore from Shackleford Banks, by Dr. Russell Coles in 1918. Coles spent many years hunting for sharks and rays in the waters off Cape Lookout in the first quarter of the twentieth century. Even today, scientists owe a huge debt to this retired tobacco farmer from Danville, Virginia, for the

work he did documenting the various species of large marine animals he personally observed.

This particular specimen turned out to be among the most interesting Coles ever studied. On June 28, 1918, he came across a large great white that had been tangled in a net near Cape Lookout. Earlier, some other fishermen from the Ocean Leather Company reported seeing an enormous shark tangled in a fishing net just offshore, but when they said the shark was as big as their twenty-five-foot-long fishing boat, Coles dismissed their story as a tall tale. But something about their story piqued his interest. Perhaps he thought back to a run-in he had in 1905 in the Lookout Bight when a twenty-footer rammed his skiff. Whatever it was, he decided to have a look.

Coles must have been used to hearing unverified reports of some really big sharks lurking offshore. Sometimes, fishermen brought back evidence to help substantiate such stories. For instance, the promoter of the North Carolina Outer Banks at the time, Aycock Brown, once reported a story of some fishermen working in the warm waters of the Gulf Stream off Cape Lookout when they hooked a great white more than thirty feet long. The shark was so big that it could not be hauled aboard the commercial shark fishing boat that caught it, so the fishermen were unable to prove the veracity of their story. They did, however, extract some teeth from the giant shark, and, according to Brown, they measured a remarkable four inches long.

Though the 1918 great white was not quite a thirty-footer, Coles found it to be among the largest he had personally seen, and on closer investigation, he realized the fishermen's description of the large shark was remarkably accurate. "My carefully noted observations justify the following claim of dimensions for it," wrote Coles. "Length, 22 ft.; head, larger than 50 gallon barrel; mouth, 3 ft. wide; circumference at arm-pit of pectoral, 18 ft.; length of pectoral, 6 ft.; width of pectoral, 3½ ft.; dorsal, not seen; width at caudal notch, origin of tail, 20 in.; width of tail, 7 ft.; weight, over 2 tons."

Most people to this day do not understand the significance of Coles's detailed calculations, as this places the shark among the largest great whites ever seen anywhere in the world. For instance, the famed "Monstruo de Cojimar," which was caught off the coast of Cuba in the summer of 1945, is acknowledged by most authorities to have been one of the largest great whites ever caught, with a total length of twenty-one feet. The longest accurately measured and independently verified great white ever recorded was taken off the coast of Malta in 1987. It measured twenty-three and a half feet long.

Controversy surrounds efforts to accurately measure fully mature *Carcharodon carcharias*, with many scientists using arcane formulae to tear down one case and build up another. The largest great whites ever reported were truly remarkable fish if the reports are anywhere near accurate. One specimen from False Bay, South Africa, was reputed to be forty-three feet long. Another large great white shark, this one caught in 1930 off Grand Manan Island in the Bay of Fundy between New Brunswick and Nova Scotia, was reputed to be thirty-six and a half feet long. The sizes of these enormous sharks were never independently verified, and through the years, they have been disputed by researchers.

Since the giant great white shark escaped from the net before Coles could extract a tooth or cut off a fin, he was unable to bring anything tangible back from the Cape Lookout specimen. He no doubt would have forwarded this evidence to one of the museums he regularly sent materials from his studies in these waters. We are fortunate that he escaped injury (or worse) when the shark wrestled free, as Coles took the time to publish his account of the large sharks he found there off Shackleford Banks in June 1918. Coles's meticulous work helps separate this particular shark from other legendary monstrous great whites encountered off the Carolina coast and elsewhere.

Newspaper columnist Billy Arthur wrote about a record-breaking white shark caught along the shores of Cape Lookout during the waning months of World War II. Arthur quoted Captain Jimmie Guthrie's note from Harker's Island (the original is from the *Beaufort News* but does not give any bibliographic details of the original article) chronicling a battle with a large female great white that occurred in March 1945 at Cape Lookout.

> *The boys, being the kind that would not quit, harpooned it near the fore fin with a real lance used primarily for whaling…The little pilot boats were cleared for real action…and well they were, for the whole hook was a light*

blaze with a whirl of salt water way up the air, the men cheering, the real war was on in Cape Lookout Hook.

When 5 hours had past [sic] by, the greatest of all sea monsters was taken ashore, it proved to be a shark 30 feet long, and the oil in the liver alone filled six kerosene barrels, its teeth were two inches long, it could easily swallow a fish barrel and weigh 3 tons.

The same shark, due to exertion and fighting, excitement and so forth, gave birth to 6 small sharks, six feet in length.

It is too bad Coles passed away several years before this memorable shark was landed, as there were no naturalists on hand to study the shark or take down any important details—at least none whose data has been preserved.

Scientists soon forgot about the gravid female taken by the crew off Shackleford Banks, using their improvised whaling implements to capture their fish. By the latter half of the twentieth century, scientists were still trying to pin down such basic questions like whether great whites give birth in this region of the world or have some mysterious birthing grounds in more remote reaches of the globe.

Today, we have a better understanding of the vital place apex predators such as sharks play in the marine ecosystem, thanks in no small part to

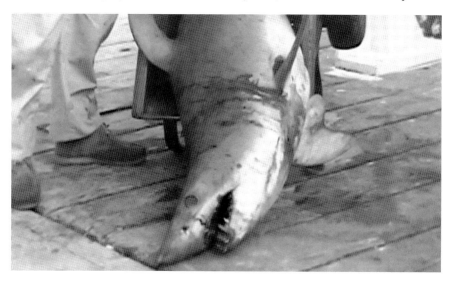

Though this shark was at first misidentified as a porbeagle shark, Dr. Frank Schwartz's examination of its serrated teeth in the lower jaw proved this shark, caught at the wreck of the *Atlas* tanker in 1980, was in fact a juvenile great white. *Photograph courtesy of Dr. Frank Schwartz, UNC Institute of Marine Sciences.*

Coles's fieldwork. Studies of sharks over the past century have shown that, in many cases, sharks employ complex thought processes to successfully acquire their prey in virtually every ecosystem on Earth. To claim that they are bungling, lovable oafs aimlessly passing from one meal to the next does a terrible disservice to both scientists and other researchers who are searching for a truer understanding of interactions between people and the underwater world.

One way in which we gain valuable insights into the lives of large sharks is by tracking their movements through the seas. Some sharks can even be tracked in real time, while others require the much more time-consuming method of using tags that pop off the shark after a certain period. The knowledge gained confirms that large sharks, especially great whites, continue to live in areas along the North Carolina coast, some passing through on their peregrinations through the oceans and others spending their lives just offshore. The work of scientists affiliated with the National Marine Fisheries Service's Cooperative Shark Tagging Program, as well as important early twenty-first-century studies made by OCEARCH, has gone a long way in helping people get a more balanced understanding of the lives of these creatures than the studies of dead animals ever allowed.

3

HINTS OF EARLY SHARK ATTACKS

Despite the fact that people traveled on a variety of watercraft, such as canoes, sailboats, timber rafts and periaugers, on waters in close proximity with sharks, there were no reports of sharks attacking individuals during the colonial period. This seems a bit hard to believe, considering the total shark population would have been much higher in the 1600s and 1700s than it was after people started harvesting large numbers of sharks in the shark fishing operations that moved into the region around the turn of the twentieth century.

We know that Natives fished for sharks, especially along the Outer Banks, as John White drew a watercolour of several Natives fishing from a canoe in waters filled with several species of fish, including sharks, off Roanoke Island in the late 1500s.

Years later, naturalists like John Lawson and Dr. John Brickell documented sharks being part of the marine ichthyofauna in the waters of North Carolina, but neither mentions any sort of misadventures between the colonists and their Native neighbours and sharks. Both include fascinating details about how people caught sharks in the early 1700s: "Of these there are two sorts; one call'd *Paracooda*-Noses; the other Shovel-Noses; they cannot take their Prey before they turn themselves on their Backs; wherefore some Negros and others that can swim and dive well go naked into the Water, with a Knife in their Hand, and fight the Shark, and very commonly kill him or wound him so that he turns Tail and runs away." Lawson goes on to point out that colonists were already utilizing

Above: Theodor de Bry's engraving of John White's watercolor shows Natives off Roanoke fishing for a variety of fish, including sharks. *Image courtesy of the Library of Congress.*

Opposite: An angler along the Outer Banks with a hammerhead shark. *Photograph by Danny Oden, courtesy of the Outer Banks History Center.*

sharks as a valuable natural resource. "Their Livers make good Oil to dress Leather withal; the Bones found in their Head are said to hasten the Birth and ease the Stone by bringing it away. Their Meat is eaten in scarce times; but I never could away with it, though a great Lover of Fish. Their Back-Bone is of one entire Thickness. Of the Bones, or Joints, I have known Buttons made, which serve well enough in scarce Times, and remote Places." Thus, sharks, as a valuable commodity that later drew shark hunters to the southern Outer Banks, were already being exploited.

Brickell, writing in 1737, expanded on Lawson's account, providing several unique details that he had uncovered while in the colony.

The Shark, whereof there are two sorts. The first is called the Paracoda-Noses, the other the Shovel-Noses: Both these are very large, bold, voracious and dangerous Fishes, especially to those that have the misfortune to fall over board. It is reported that they will follow Ships for Hours together, and if either Man or Dog or any other living Animal happen to fall into the Water, they immediately seize and snap in two, having exceeding sharp, and several Rows of Teeth in their Heads: Some of them are so large that they

are said to weigh about four thousand Weight. They are easily caught with a Bait but can never take their Prey till they turn themselves on their Backs, wherefore some Negroes and others that can swim and dive well go naked into the Waters with a Knife in their Hands, and fight them, and commonly kill, or wound him so that he turns Tail and runs away. Their Flesh is eaten in time of scarcity but is not very palatable, having a strong fishy taste. Their Liver makes good Oil to dress Leather with, and the Bones found in their Head, are said to hasten the Birth and ease the Stone by bringing it away. Their Back-bone is of one entire thickness, having many Joints in it, whereof I have known Buttons made by the Sailors and others that live in those remote Places. Gillius says that the People of Marseilles told him that they had caught one of them, in which they found a Man armed with a Coat of Mail.

Brickell next related a tragic episode with which he was familiar of people dealing with sharks on the high seas much closer to home than France.

August 1730, a Sloop sailed from North Carolina, bound to the Island in the West Indies, and after four Days sailing from the Bar, was most unfortunately over-set, and all the Crew, except the Master, two Sailors, and one Negroe, were drowned, these being upon Deck at the time when this misfortune happened and had the good providence to get upon the Keel of the Vessel, where they remained twenty one Days and then were taken up by a Vessel trading to Europe; having neither Water or any other Necessaries to support Nature but by Gods Providence, the Negroe killed a Shark, whereon they lived and was the only support they had during the said time, which was confirmed by the Master in his Letter from London to his Friends in North Carolina.

Brickell's account demonstrates that people along the coast were learning to deal with the sharks that were a constant companion to any who traveled along the coastal waters of North Carolina.

The large number of shipwrecks along the North Carolina made these waters part of the infamous "Graveyard of the Atlantic." Scores of ships went down just offshore, and many unwary mariners no doubt experienced many of the same horrors their later counterparts did on ships like the *Libertad* during the twentieth century (discussed later). Unfortunately, there were no spotter aircraft or diesel-powered rescue ships waiting around to try to whisk people to safety. Sometimes, ships came across evidence of shipwrecks where sharks had been at work on the remains of a hapless crewman or passenger.

Oftentimes, macabre mementos of these offshore tragedies washed up along the beaches after a storm passed up the coast. Take, for instance, the poor woman who strapped herself to the mast of a now all but forgotten ship that was battered to pieces by the waves during a storm off Bogue Banks in 1875.

> *The body of a young woman was found washed on the beach near Fort Macon on Wednesday of last week. It is supposed that she was lost from some unfortunate vessel. There was nothing by which it could be identified. The head and right leg were gone, believed to have been demolished by a shark. A friend writes us that the clothing consisted of a neat worsted garment, flannel undershirt and skirt, a calico wrapper and waterproof cloak, muslin drawers and cloth laced boots, no. 4, with rubber overshoes. On the hand was a plain gold ring. There was also a rope fastened around her waist, by which she had been fastened to a mast or some kind of floating timber. The ring and the other articles were retained by the officer in charge of the fort for recognition (anonymous, 1875).*

Scenes such as this one were regular reminders of the dangers lurking beneath the waves offshore.

We can learn more about similar travails met by mariners who were passing along this stretch of coast by looking at the experiences of the crew of the brig *Richmond*. On September 18, 1849, someone living near Cape Hatteras brought a peculiar item to the offices of the *Old North State* newspaper in Raleigh. The item had been washed up on the beach following a fierce hurricane that passed up the coast that summer—it was literally a message in a bottle. From what they were able to decipher, the letter was written in haste, the captain and crew knowing the end was near. They wanted to let their families as well as the owners of the ship know what had become of them. The letter reads:

> *The Brig* Richmond *of Halifax is now in the heaviest gale of wind ever experienced on the high seas. She has lost both masts close to the deck and is expected to go down every moment, having a hole stove in bows by the mast bumping against her. We cannot survive more than an hour. No boat can live in a sea like this. We have made rafts and intended to try our fate: for while there is life, there is hope. Hoping this will be received and*

Robert Keller with a record-breaking dusky shark landed off Jennette's Pier in Nag's Head. *Photograph courtesy of North Carolina Archives and History.*

our melancholy fate (that is to be) be reported silently and carefully to our friends: and that you may put this in the papers to let the owners, Messrs Fairbanks and Allison, know the loss of the vessel.

The document was signed by Captain George Vernum, who added a postscript: "The sharks are at this moment in numbers about us. From this guess if we will be long on a raft. These gents will try it also. Good bye" (anonymous, 1849). There is no further mention of Vernum and his men or whether they survived plunging into the shark-infested waters, but it is doubtful they survived their ordeal much longer than it took to put the bottle into the water.

The offshore waters of North Carolina are home to one particularly dangerous species of shark: the oceanic whitetip. Prowling the open seas well offshore, *Carcharhinus longimanus* have gained a bad reputation for being a threat to victims of tragedies on the high seas. Some oceanic whitetips grow as much as thirteen feet long. Most, however, are believed to be around seven or eight feet long. They are so named because of the white tips on their tails and fins, which stand out in contrast to their brownish colour.

Since they are a pelagic species that inhabits the offshore realm, they are seldom seen along North Carolina's beaches, but on those unfortunate occasions when an airplane goes down in the ocean or a ship sinks, these large sharks turn out in force to feast on the victims. The sharks often live in large schools. According to Bright (2000), a school consisting of hundreds of these sharks was seen off the Massachusetts coast in 1941. "According to deep-sea fishermen, the further from land they are seen, the more numerous they become." Oceanic whitetips are found in the world's oceans well offshore. Though some occasionally find their way as far north as Canada, they prefer areas where water temperature stays warmer than seventy degrees Fahrenheit.

These sharks are found in the waters off the North Carolina coast, but to see them, one normally has to head for deep water. Schwartz and Burgess (1975) observed that they are found in the area all year long "in waters deeper than 183 meters (100 femtometres)." They are most often seen near the edge of the continental shelf, especially from Hatteras northward.

4

EARLY SHARK ATTACKS

The previous section of this book concentrates on several episodes that demonstrate people and sharks have been interacting along the coast of North Carolina for many years. But documented attacks do not appear in any literature during North Carolina's first two centuries of settlement as a British colony. Since the colony played a key role in Britain's maritime-based empire, perhaps colonial officials felt it was not wise to let word spread about one of the dangers awaiting settlers once they arrived in the New World.

June 1812
Brunswick County, Species Uncertain

The earliest documented fatal shark attack in North Carolina occurred in the waters of the Cape Fear River off Smithville (modern Southport) in June 1812, when one of the sailors attached to *Gun Boat Number 7* was killed by a shark while swimming in the river. A very brief note (anonymous, 1812) gives few details of the incident: "On the 26th ult. part of the crew of Gun-Boat No. 7, went on shore in a boat for the purpose of bathing, when one of the best swimmers suddenly sunk and rose no more, supposed to be taken by a shark—a very large one was frequently seen that day."

We do not, unfortunately, have any details about the shark in question or any sketches to give further clues. Some might be tempted to implicate a

The waters near the mouth of the Cape Fear River are home to many large species of sharks capable of doing serious damage to a human. Here off Southport is where North Carolina's earliest shark fatality occurred in 1812.

bull shark, *Carcharhinus leucas*, as the culprit, but there are numerous species of sharks found in the estuarian reaches of the Cape Fear River, with the waters between Wilmington and Bald Head Island having a high enough salinity content to be home to numerous species of sharks. The largest species of sharks in the world, the whale shark (*Rhincodon typus*), is found in North Carolina waters, with a specimen once found stranded on a sandbar between Fort Fisher and Southport. Whale sharks do not feed on prey as large as humans, however, and are thus not responsible for any of the attacks mentioned in this publication. The species responsible was most likely a great white, a tiger shark or a bull shark, all of which frequent the waters of the Cape Fear River.

White sharks in the Cape Fear River? Some might think such a claim is a tall tale or a legend from days of yore. But *Carcharodon carcharias* are part of the marine fauna of the lower reaches of the river and have been seen with more regularity than some might want to admit.

Great whites have been observed close to the beaches along the Cape Fear coast. For instance, on April 27, 1985, a great white was caught two miles

Remains of a whale shark found in the Cape Fear River in 1934. *An H.H. Brimley photograph, courtesy of North Carolina Archives and History.*

off Wrightsville Beach, roughly a mile north of the Wrightsville Jetty. At the time, Dean Jordan, Hubert Jordan and William Sullivan were on a fishing trip, working the waters between Cape Fear and Winyah Bay. They landed several sharks, including a large tiger shark, but the most interesting fish they caught was a large shark they believed to be a great white. This fish was an immature female that measured seven feet, eight inches long and weighed 250 pounds.

Since none of the three fishermen had ever seen a great white in person before, they were not certain about the identity of the shark. After returning to their home port of Georgetown, South Carolina, they contacted the South Carolina Department of Natural Resources to identify the fish. Don Hammond, a fisheries biologist with the department, investigated the shark and positively identified it as a great white.

Another instance of someone spotting a great white near shore along the Cape Fear coast occurred on May 18, 1996, when two passengers aboard jet skis encountered an enormous great white just off Wrightsville Beach. The people who were on board the jet ski believed the shark was approximately twenty feet long. They were sure it was a great white, as they got a good look at the shark's distinctive teeth. The great white made what the couple perceived to be a few threatening gestures, which prompted them to leave the area with much haste. There was another report of a large great white in the area that same day. According to Dr. Schwartz, this shark was spotted by some divers who were moored off the testing buoy near 5-Mile Reef. Whether this was the same great white as the one encountered by the small craft closer to Wrightsville Beach is unknown.

Great whites have been spotted swimming not just off Cape Fear but inside the river itself. For example, in the summer of 1998, John Woods III was fishing from his nineteen-and-a-half-foot-long boat in the main channel of the Cape Fear River between Bald Head Island and Southport. There, he caught three small sharks ranging in size from a foot to a foot and a half long. Much blood was spilled as he attempted to release the third shark, and as Woods leaned over the side of his boat to wash his hands, he noticed that he was not alone. "I looked down into the water, and less than a foot away from my bloody hands was an eyeball the size of a saucer looking back at me," said Woods. "I did see the gray tops and sides and the tell-tale white bottom as he passed the boat at a forty-five-degree angle. He must have come up behind the boat to avoid hitting it. His tail came slightly out of the water before he went back down, and I left the area! His eye was four and half to five inches across."

By Woods's reckoning, this was an enormous great white. "I watched the animal's front end pass the front of my boat (nineteen and a half feet). Then

A great white shark caught in 1985 off Wrightsville Beach by Dean Jordan, Hubert Jordan and Danny Sullivan. *Photograph by Don Hammond, South Carolina Department of Natural Resources.*

I looked back, and I could see its tail…still four feet beyond the back of my boat. This animal had to be between twenty-five and thirty feet in length."

Later that same year, another great white was spotted in the inshore waters near Cape Fear. This one was found floating dead on the water by some fishermen in the Intracoastal Waterway near Wilmington on December 12, 1998. They reported their find to the Wrightsville Coast Guard Station. Fifteen coast guardsmen hauled the massive shark out of the water near the end of Bozeman Road, not far from channel marker 154 between Masonboro Island and the mainland. Parker was called in from the aquarium at Fort Fisher to have a look at this large shark.

"We had a fourteen-foot-seven-inch-long total length female white shark," said Parker. "It was very large, nine feet in girth around the pectorals. Her mouth was large enough to have bitten me in half if necessary. Once I opened her up, she could have swallowed me whole. She was full of squid and was not in chasing mammals or anything of that nature—or even larger fish."

Upon further investigation, Parker found that the shark had liver damage. He suspects that the shark was shot after raiding someone's tuna catch. Seeing this great white was a rare treat for Parker, who spends much of his time researching the various shark species that prowl the shores of southeastern North Carolina. "This is the only great white I have encountered. It's the largest one that has been landed along the North Carolina coast since 1986."

The presence of great white sharks in the Cape Fear River is a known fact, documented by both scientists and laymen alike. Based on tracking data and human observation, we know that great white sharks do indeed leave the ocean depths and head up rivers. These large sharks frequent the mouth of the Cape Fear River, especially in the lower reaches between Bald Head Island and Southport. Thus, we cannot rule out *Carcharodon carcharias* as the culprit of this early fatal attack off Southport.

SEPTEMBER 1839
OCRACOKE/HYDE COUNTY, SPECIES UNCERTAIN

In the fall of 1839, Francis Dixon, a pilot from Ocracoke, had a run-in with a large shark while fishing in Pamlico Sound. He and four companions set their nets in the waters of the sound, hoping to catch a good supply of fish for their families, but they were interrupted by a large shark raiding their

Sharks were a constant hazard for fishermen wading in shallow water, tending to their nets, such as these mullet fishermen working in Core Sound in 1907. *North Carolina Geological Survey photograph.*

net and stealing the fish they had caught. Four of the men scrambled for the safety of their vessel, but one of their companions was made of sterner stuff. As they looked on, they saw Dixon was not headed for the boat but was making his way to deeper water in an effort to defend their hard-earned catch from the ravenous shark.

> *The daring pilot making his way toward the seine, rolling up his sleeves and screaming, "The —ed creature should not tear up his net in that fashion." Up to his word, with clenched fists, he pounced upon his adversary. His shark ship, though conscious of his power, seemed unwilling to risk an engagement on this shoal and made for deeper water, which, in spite of his fatigue, he reached and commenced his fight by plunging and rolling entirely over, yet his antagonist with his left arm and legs retained his hold, aware that the loss of it would be certain death.*

Dixon held on for dear life, trying with his free hand to punch away at the shark, but his blows were of little effect, as the water absorbed much of the power of his punches. After several minutes, Dixon remembered he had a small pocketknife with him and reached into his pocket to pull out what must have seemed, at the time, to be a woefully inadequate blade for the task at hand. He slashed methodically at his antagonist's throat. The shark began to weaken and finally died. Dixon dragged his bloody trophy toward his companions, who had watched the action from the safety of their small boat. A correspondent (anonymous, 1839) reported, "Dixon alone had survived the battle. The shark measured nine feet, two inches."

Dixon's shark was most likely a bull or a great white, though tiger sharks cannot be totally ruled out if the water was still warm enough for them to be hanging around in Pamlico Sound that late in the year.

OCTOBER 1855
DARE COUNTY, SPECIES UNKNOWN

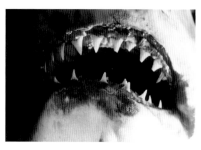

Top: A great white shark caught by Glen Hopkins off Drum Inlet in 1996. *Photograph by Jim Francesconi, North Carolina Division of Marine Fisheries.*

Bottom: A close-up view of Glen Hopkins's great white shark landed at Ocracoke. *Photograph by Jim Francesconi, North Carolina Division of Marine Fisheries.*

On September 30, 1855, the *William Penn* ran aground on a shoal just off Cape Hatteras. Before the ship was beaten to pieces by the raging surf with people on the shore unable to come to their assistance, the crew managed to prepare rafts to take their chances in the deeper waters farther offshore. At least four men were killed, but exactly how many is uncertain. The captain's wife, identified simply as Mrs. Cole, was accompanying her husband on the voyage and was one of those onboard the raft. She later penned a brief account of their ordeal off the North Carolina coast, mentioning that sharks circled the raft on which she was floating for several hours, but they held off on attacking those aboard until they were being rescued by the schooner *Marcus*. She wrote, "We bade adieu to our raft that was then surrounded by turtles, dolphins, and sharks too ravenous to wait their time. A shark bit one of the sailors that had dropped his foot over the side" (anonymous, 1855). She never elaborated about the extent of the sailor's injuries or whether they proved to be fatal.

It is difficult to pin down exactly which species of shark was responsible for biting the sailor from the *William Penn* on the leg. Blue sharks, *Prionace glauca*, are prime suspects. They are medium-sized sharks known to be very shy when confronting their victims, sometimes waiting almost to the point of their victim's death before moving in for the kill.

5

MID-NINETEENTH-CENTURY SHARK ATTACKS

As the nineteenth century moved onward, an increasing number of people found themselves spending time outdoors. This was not just recreational, but many people engaged in military pursuits along the shores of the southeastern reaches of the country. Sharks no doubt took advantage of all these activities to pick off easy meals, but military authorities, both in the North and South, kept a tight lid on such incidents, lest they have trouble recruiting people to serve in the ranks of their respective units.

October 1864
Carteret County, Species Uncertain

On October 2, 1864, a steamer went ashore along the Core Banks between Cape Lookout and Ocracoke. Details of the episode are sketchy thanks to wartime secrecy, but there were multiple fatalities due to sharks feeding on some of the survivors as they tried to flee the ship and head for shore. Press reports (anonymous, 1864) noted, "A new U.S. steam transport from Boston to Key West went ashore on Sunday the 2nd inst. nine miles north of Cape Lookout. She had bilged and would be a total lost. She had four hundred seamen on board, some of whom, while landing, were capsized, and 5 were destroyed by sharks."

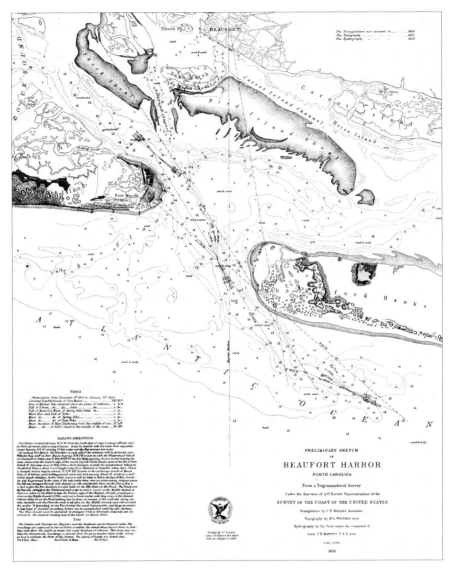

A chart of Beaufort Inlet, prepared by Lieutenant John N. Maffitt in 1851. Note the location of Shark Shoals between Beaufort and Fort Macon. *NMFS Maps*.

Multiple species were no doubt responsible for the attacks, with bodies in the water attracting hungry sharks from far and wide to the Core Banks, especially cool-water sharks like great whites.

June 1870
Brunswick County, Species Uncertain

Almost sixty years after the first documented Cape Fear River shark fatality, in nearly the same spot, another individual was attacked by a shark but had a much less tragic outcome than the earlier victim. On July 26, 1870, several members of Battery G, Fourth Artillery, were swimming in the Cape Fear River opposite Fort Johnson when bugler Giles Gordon had his foot seized by a shark. Shortly thereafter, a witness (anonymous, 1870) described the scene: "When a shark first seized the bugler, it drew him beneath the surface of the water; but, by the violent exertions of the disentangled leg, he tore the other foot from the grasp of the terrible monster and swam a few feet to the wharf, when he was assisted out of the water and taken to the hospital."

Fortunately for the victim, medical attention was only a short distance away. The post surgeon was able to dress the wound and save the man's mangled foot. Giles, who, at the time, was being discharged from the service, as his enlistment term had expired, convalesced at Fort Johnston before heading home.

There is no way to know for certain the exact species involved in this attack, since there were no drawings of the shark or any teeth left behind in a local museum. Most would contend that since the attack took place in the river, it must have been a bull shark, which are frequently found in freshwater rivers and lakes. However, as explained earlier, the salinity of the water of the Cape Fear River off Southport is high enough for other large species of sharks, like great whites and tiger sharks, to be able to feed and explore in these waters without suffering any ill effects to their health.

Tiger sharks, *Galeocerdo cuvier*, are one of the most dangerous shark species swimming in the world's oceans. Many shark experts throughout the world categorize tiger sharks as more of a threat than even the legendary great white, since tiger sharks inhabit the warm, shallow waters where humans are known to congregate. However, according to the data collected by the University of Florida's International Shark Attack File, through 2021, tiger sharks were responsible for 102 nonfatal shark attacks and 36 fatal attacks, second only to the great white. Tiger sharks are considered to be one of the three most dangerous shark species found in the waters off North Carolina.

These large sharks are fairly easy to identify in the water. The upper portion of the tiger shark's body ranges in color from gray to brown, while the portion underneath is white, gray or even yellow. When young, a tiger shark's skin is covered with black blotches. As the shark matures, the blotches stretch into long, faint stripes that resemble the stripes of a tiger, hence the name. They are the largest members of a family of sharks known as requiem sharks. Tiger sharks, on average, are believed to grow to somewhere between thirteen and fifteen feet long. But some tiger sharks are reputed to measure in excess of twenty feet long and weigh more than a ton. Some remarkable tiger sharks have been landed here in the waters off North Carolina, especially in the area between Cape Fear and Little River Inlet.

Thanks to shark tagging studies, we now know that tiger sharks can travel great distances—in some instances swimming thousands of miles to waters off the continents bordering the Atlantic Ocean. Researchers from the Cooperative Shark Tagging Program (1997) noted, "These fish showed movements from North Carolina to south and east of the Flemish Cap and west of the Spanish Sahara; from Georgia to the Cape Verde Islands; from Bimini to New York." One of these well-traveled tiger sharks was caught and released off Cape Hatteras in January 1996. The shark turned up again in the summer of 1997 1,549 nautical miles away.

The earliest reliably documented account of a tiger shark landed in North Carolina waters dates to 1885. On July 30 that year, J.N. Maffitt and J.A. Corbett were fishing off the mouth of the Cape Fear River when they spotted a large shark. One of the men had brought along a rifle and used it to shoot the shark. After bringing the shark back to Southport and examining its body, it was determined that the men had killed a tiger shark. Bill Reaves (1994) later noted that the shark was "10 feet long and 5 feet in circumference and weighed 400 pounds." The men skinned the shark and kept its skin as a souvenir of the encounter.

Though they are definitely a threat to humans, tiger sharks appear to be far more dangerous to other sharks than to people. On numerous occasions in the waters off North Carolina, tiger sharks have been seen engaging in acts of cannibalism against other sharks, including other tiger sharks.

Lewis Radcliffe of the U.S. Marine Fisheries Laboratory in Beaufort, North Carolina, witnessed a cannibalistic attack from the deck of his boat, the *Fish Hawk*, back in August 1914. While in the Fort Macon Channel of Beaufort Inlet, Radcliffe noticed a small school of these fish swimming around his boat, so he decided to try to catch one. He quickly hauled in three tiger sharks, measuring $8\frac{3}{8}$ feet, $10\frac{1}{2}$ feet and $9\frac{1}{16}$ feet, respectively. As he was hoisting the third catch on board, another tiger shark rushed up and tried to deprive him of his prize.

Radcliffe, in 1914, wrote of the incident:

> *About this time, a shark, larger than any of those taken, swam up to the one hanging from the boom, and raising its head partly out of the water, seized the dead shark by the throat. As it did so, the captain of the Fish Hawk began shooting at it with a .32-caliber revolver as rapidly as he could take aim. The shots seemed only to infuriate the shark, and it shook the dead one so viciously as to make it seem doubtful whether the boom would withstand its onslaught. Finally, it tore a very large section of the unfortunate's belly, tearing out and devouring the whole liver, leaving a gaping hole across the entire width of the body large enough to permit a small child to easily enter the body cavity. At this instant, one of the bullets struck a vital spot, and after a lively struggle on the part of the launch's crew, a rope was secured around its tail.*

Upon his return to Beaufort, Radcliffe laid out his sharks for measurement and study. His fourth and final tiger shark measured twelve feet long. Inside its stomach were forty pounds of the undigested remains of the third tiger shark's liver. Inside one of the other tiger sharks was a rat, while another had the remains of an unidentified shark.

Tiger sharks have a reputation for not being too finicky when it comes to getting a meal. British author Michael Bright (2000), who refers to tiger sharks as "the ocean's dustbin with fins," compiled the following list of items that have been consumed by tiger sharks:

> *At one time or another, rubber tyres, a roll of tar paper, a roll of chicken wire, a bag of potatoes, a sack of coal, beer bottles, plastic bags, a tom-tom drum, pork chops, hamburgers, lobsters, trousers, horns of deer, cloth rags, glass bottles, leather shoes, tennis shoes, sea snakes, squid, unopened tins of green peas and salmon, cigarette tins, an artillery shell casing, bag of money, explosives, pet cats and dogs, parts of dolphins, porpoises and whales, other sharks, stingrays, and a variety of land and sea birds have been found in the stomachs of tiger sharks.*

Noted shark hunter Russell Coles believed that such claims may in fact be an oversimplification. He captured a tiger shark off Cape Lookout on July 5, 1918, that measured twelve feet, six inches in length. He had no way of weighing the shark there on the beach, but he was very impressed with the shark's size. As a testimony to the size of the shark, Coles observed, "I weigh

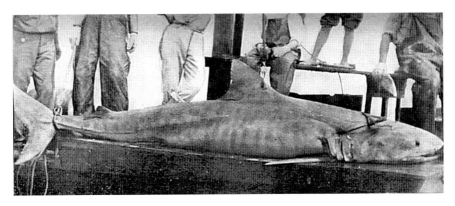

A tiger shark caught by Russell Coles along the beach at Cape Lookout. *A National Marine Fisheries Service photograph.*

275 lbs. and have a 52-inch waist, yet I passed through its jaws, which I have nicely cleaned."

Coles made a detailed examination of the shark, making special note of the contents of its stomach. He wrote, "Stomach contained most varied assortment of food that I ever found in any shark, consisting of parts of three large stone crabs, one bird, the small diver called locally water witch, and other unidentified substances." He found interesting things in the stomachs of other tiger sharks he examined in the summer of 1918 at Cape Lookout, including the entire body of large loggerhead turtle, complete with its shell, inside a tiger shark that measured seven feet, nine inches long. But Coles did not ascribe to the theory that tiger sharks were indiscriminate scavengers.

> *Probably tiger sharks will use as food, when hungry, any creature which they find moving in the water, for which reason they must be dangerous as maneaters; but I do not regard them as nearly so dangerous as a white shark which has once acquired the habit of eating human flesh. While it is not fastidious, I have no evidence as yet that even the tiger shark will eat unclean food, and in my opinion, the sharks which eat garbage or putrid matter are exceptional individuals, which, through some accident, have acquired the habit.*

Tiger sharks are frequent visitors to the Cape Fear River, as the waters warm in the summer months as far upriver as Snow's Cut and the Intracoastal Waterway. Thus, the attack could have been made by any of the larger sharks found off the Cape Fear River in the summer months.

June 1876
Carteret County, Species Uncertain

On the morning of June 11, 1876, on the eve of the centennial of the United States gaining its independence, a shark killed a boy who was swimming in the waters of Bogue Sound, adjacent to Fort Macon. The boy, whose name was not recorded, was a family member of one of the soldiers serving at the fort. A press report (anonymous, 1876) noted:

> *We learn through a gentleman from Fort Macon that on Sunday last, one of the sergeants at the Fort lost his son in a horrible manner. The little boy was in surf-bathing in the rear of the Fort when he suddenly disappeared from sight, and from the commotion made in the water and the nonappearance of even the least vestige of the boy, it was presumed that a shark had taken him. The mother of the little fellow was lying very low in one of the dwellings at the fort, and for fear the shock would result in her death, the horrible news was not taken to her.*

The sound-side beach at Fort Macon, where one of the children of the fort's garrison was killed by a shark in June 1876.

There are too few details related to allow for a positive identification of the shark involved. Several species of sharks large enough to kill and consume a human are present in Bogue Sound during the late spring and early summer. Not only are great whites still in the area, but the waters have usually warmed up enough that bull sharks, tiger sharks and hammerheads are able to return to the inshore waters as well.

6

SHARK ATTACKS OF
THE LATE NINETEENTH CENTURY

As the century wound down following the end of the War Between the States, North Carolina experienced some of its most gruesome shark attacks. Thanks to an increase in commerce and expanding affluence, working people began to have more leisure time and, thus, opportunities to spend time at places like the beach. This brought more people into the surf zone, putting humans in places where sharks had, for millennia, been feeding.

As with earlier attacks, it is virtually impossible today to figure out the exact species responsible for most of these attacks. No drawings of the sharks or the wounds they left behind survive today to help us decipher what occurred.

JULY 1879
CARTERET COUNTY, SPECIES UNCERTAIN

One of the most tragic shark attacks documented in North Carolina's history occurred in the summer of 1879 in the waters of Bogue Sound. Captain Appleton Oaksmith left Beaufort on the morning of July 4 on his small sailboat, headed to Morehead City with his six children to buy provisions and to swing by Fort Macon to enjoy the Independence Day festivities. Sometime around 2:00 p.m., Oaksmith decided it was time to head home, as a thunderstorm was brewing, kicking up the winds. Before they made it back, however, the winds began swirling about, catching the sail awkwardly, flipping the boat over and depositing its passengers into the sound. An eyewitness (W.G.T., 1879) to the event in Beaufort described what happened:

> *Just before reaching this point, the boat being heavily loaded, he gibed without lowering the sail, and the boat at once turned over, and the whole crew were thrown to the mercy of the swelling tide. The father and two sons were saved, but one of the ladies has not yet been found, though the boats have been hunting for them all the evening. The other grown young lady, two little girls and the younger boy were brought back ashore, all apparently dead, but by quick and constant medical effort, the little boy was brought to life and says the last time he saw his sister, a big fish had her. It is supposed that a shark captured and devoured the body.*

Captain Appleton Oaksmith lost two daughters to sharks during a boating mishap between Fort Macon and Beaufort. *Photograph courtesy of North Carolina Archives and History.*

Another correspondent (anonymous, 1879) provided a few extra details about the accident, including the names of two of the girls who were killed, Bessie and Corrine, both of whom regularly contributed literary items to the *Farmer & Mechanic* newspaper. "By some means (an unskillful attempt to 'gibe' it is said), the frail craft was capsized and its freight thrown into the angry waves. Miss Bessie disappeared first, being struck by the sail and dragged down, it's said, by a big shark." In addition to Oaksmith's two daughters who were taken by the sharks, two others drowned before the sharks killed them, and his young son nearly died as well.

Oaksmith led a colorful life, including serving a stint as a Nicaraguan filibuster in the 1850s and blockade running during the War Between the States. After the war, he served a term in the North Carolina General Assembly as the representative from Carteret County in the 1874–75 session while engaging in several land development schemes along the Bogue Banks. His political enemies went so far as to claim Oaksmith had intentionally drowned his daughters in the sad affair, but eyewitness accounts argue against this being anything more than a tragic boating accident.

The waters of Bogue Sound between Fort Macon and Beaufort, where sharks killed Corrine and Bessie Oaksmith during a boating accident that claimed the lives of four of Captain Appleton Oaksmith's children in July 1879.

Despite the widespread coverage this attack received in the state's press, none of the pieces written about the story give any details about the sharks that killed the Oaksmith girls off Beaufort.

AUGUST 1881
DARE COUNTY, SPECIES UNCERTAIN

Just a few years later, another fatal shark attack occurred in the waters of North Carolina, this time farther up the coast along the northern Outer Banks off Dare County. Details are sparse, but we do know that in August 1881, nineteen-year-old Frank Gordon Hines was killed by a shark. A contemporary press account (anonymous, 1881) noted, "The general impression is that he was struck by a shark while bathing in the surf."

Hines was a native of Edenton and was a member of St. Paul's Episcopal Church, where parish records indicate he lost his life on August 21, 1881, and was buried four days later on August 25. Unpublished supplemental materials for the church records compiled by Elizabeth Van Moore note Hines was "attacked by a shark and drowned at Nag's Head."

Left: The grave of Frank Hines, who was killed by a shark at Nag's Head on August 22, 1882.

Below: Frank Hines rests under the shade of the trees beside historic St. Paul's Episcopal Church in Edenton.

Just after the turn of the century, Fred A. Olds, a writer and antiquarian who did much to preserve the history of North Carolina at the turn of the twentieth century, interviewed Bill Basnight, a noted outdoorsman who hailed from the northern Outer Banks. While discussing several of his notable hunting exploits (1906), Basnight gave some intriguing details about the remains of a person he found along the shore near Nags Head.

> *Mr. Basnight told me that he knew there were man-eating sharks along the North Carolina coast, because some twenty years ago, he found on the shore below Nag's Head the body of a young man who had suddenly disappeared while bathing on that beach the day before. He said the shark had bitten the body in the abdomen, there being the great oval marks of the many teeth, but the body was too much, for it did not bother it further after the one swift and horrible crash.*

Whether the person killed at Nag's Head who was found by Basnight was indeed Frank Hines or perhaps a heretofore undocumented shark attack fatality along the North Carolina coast remains a mystery. There are far too few details to help identify which species of shark was responsible for Hines's death.

July 1882
Jones County, Bull Shark/*Carcharhinus leucas*

William Riggs, while fishing near the mouth of Bear Creek, a tributary of the Neuse River that flows into the river a few miles upstream from New Bern, was attacked by an eight-foot-long shark while fishing in June 1882. Riggs was able to fight off the shark until his friend Hancock was able to render assistance. A press account (anonymous, 1882) gave a few details: "Mr. Wm. Riggs, of Bear Creek, was attacked while fishing a few days since by a large shark and came very near being killed, but finally succeeded, with the help of Mr. Hancock, a gentleman near him, in killing the monster and taking the gentleman in out of the wet. He measured eight feet in length—a regular man eater."

Based on the fact that Riggs was so far upriver, his attacker was no doubt a bull shark, which are numerous in the waters of Pamlico Sound and the Neuse River during the summer months.

AT MINNESOTT BEACH, ARAPAHOE, N. C.

Unidentified ladies fishing at Minnesott Beach in Pamlico County landed a young bull shark in the Neuse River. *Photograph from the Durwood Barbour Collection of North Carolina Postcards, North Carolina Collection Photographic Archives, Wilson Library, UNC– Chapel Hill.*

OCTOBER 1883
CARTERET COUNTY, GREAT WHITE SHARK/
CARCHARODON CARCHARIAS

The most famous of these nineteenth-century shark attacks was one that focused worldwide attention on the North Carolina coast in the fall of 1883 (anonymous, 1883). In September 1883, a sailing vessel known as the *Atlanta* went down in a storm on the inlet side of the Beaufort Bar. The ship's owners, hoping to save whatever they could of their valuable ship and its cargo, engaged the services of a diving crew to bring what they could back to the surface. We do not know the name of this salvage vessel nor any of the names of the crew members except for the surname of a Spanish diver, Alfetto. We would not even know his name without the encounter he had with a great white shark that nearly turned fatal.

Sometime in late October and early November 1883, Alfetto and another diver were on the bottom of the sea, hard at work on the remains of the *Atlanta*. After a few successful dives, the men decided to return to the surface

Beaufort Inlet, where the Spanish diver Alfetto was attacked and nearly killed by a great white shark in the fall of 1883.

so they could rest in their boat, which was waiting above. The Spaniard sent his companion up first and planned to follow him up to the surface once he had secured one final object. As the unnamed diver was being hauled up through the water to the surface above, he watched in horror as a large great white shark grabbed his diving partner, carrying the poor man away in its mouth. When he finally made his way back onto the boat, the diver frantically related to his shipmates what he had seen befall the Spaniard in the watery depths below. As the man finished his story, those onboard were sure that their companion would be eaten by the ravenous shark. Instead, they saw their friend surface approximately fifty yards from their boat.

He was unconscious when they reached him, but fortunately, he was still alive. He bore no wounds on his body, but his metal diving suit bore the scars of the encounter, as there were holes left behind by the shark's razor-sharp teeth. They could only guess about why the large shark had attacked their friend in the first place and then let him go. Researchers in the twentieth century conducted several tests, looking for a reliable shark repellent. One such repellent was based on copper, so perhaps the diver's copper suit was not palatable to this great white.

Alfetto slowly recovered. He spent more than a day recuperating from his ordeal before he was able to speak with his companions and tell them about what happened on the bottom of the sea in Beaufort Inlet. The following is Alfetto's first-person account of his terrifying encounter in the waters just off Fort Macon:

> As you know, we had made our fourth descent, and, while my companion clambered into the vessel, I waited on the ground till he should attach the cords to draw something out. I was just about to signal to be drawn up for a moment's rest when I noticed a shadowy body moving at some distance above me and towards me. In a moment, every fish had disappeared, the very crustacean lay still upon the sand, and the cuttle-fish scurried away as fast as they could. I was not thinking of danger, and my first thought was that it was the shadow of a passing boat. But suddenly, a feeling of terror seized me; I felt impelled to flee from something; I knew not what; a vague horror seemed grasping after me, such as a child fancies when leaving a darkened room. By this time, the shadow had come nearer and taken shape. I scarcely needed a glance to show me that it was a man-eater, and of the largest size. Had I signalled to be drawn up then, it would have been certain death. All I could do was to remain still until it left. It lay off twenty-five feet, just outside the rigging of the ship, its body motionless, its

fins barely stirring the water about its gills. It was a monster as it was, but to add to the horror, the pressure of the water upon my head made it appear as if pouring flames from its eyes and mouth, and every movement of its fins and tail seemed accompanied by a display of fireworks. I was sure the fish was thirty feet long and so near that I could see its double row of white teeth. Involuntarily, I shrank closer to the side of the vessel. But the first movement betrayed my presence. I saw the shining eyes fixed upon me; its tail quivered as it darted at me like a streak of light. I shrank closer to the side of the ship. I saw it turn on its side, its mouth open, and heard the teeth snap as it darted by me. It had missed me, but only for a moment. The sweep of its mighty tail had thrown me forward. I saw it turn, balance itself, and its tail quivered as it darted by me again. There was no escape. It turned on its back as it swooped down on me like a hawk on a sparrow. The cavernous jaws opened, and the long shining teeth grated as they closed on my metal harness. It had me. I could feel its teeth grinding upon my copper breastplate as it tried to bite me in two; for fortunately, it had caught me just across the middle, where I was best protected. Having seized me, it went tearing through the water. I could feel it bound forward at each stroke of its tail. Had it not been for my copper helmet, my head would have been torn off by the rush through the water. I was perfectly conscious, but somehow, I felt no terror at all. There was only a feeling of numbness. I wondered how long it would be before those teeth would crunch through and whether they would strike first into my back or my breast. Then I thought of Maggie and the baby and wondered who would take care of them and if she would ever know what had become of me. All these thoughts had passed through my brain in an instant, but in that time, the connecting air tube had been snapped, and my head seemed ready to burst with pressure when the monster's teeth kept crunching and grinding away upon my harness. Then I felt the cold water begin to pour in and heard the bubble, bubble, bubble, as the air escaped into the creature's mouth. I began to hear great guns and to see fireworks and rainbows and sunshine and all kinds of pretty things; then I thought I was floating away on a rosy summer cloud, dreaming to the sound of sweet music. Then all became blank. The shark might have eaten me then at his leisure, and I never would have been the wiser. Imagine my astonishment, then, when I opened my eyes on board this boat and saw you fellows around me. Yes, sir! I thought I was dead and eaten up, sure.

A few years later, in 1888, the crew of Captain Willis's whaling crew, while operating off Shackleford Banks, had their run-in with a giant great white shark they inadvertently caught just off the beach. There are some who have suggested that this was probably the same shark that nearly killed the Spanish diver Alfetto, but our knowledge of shark behavior and migration patterns argues that such an encounter is unlikely, though not totally impossible.

So far, the misadventures of Alfetto and his diving companion in Beaufort Inlet off Fort Macon remain the earliest documented great white shark attack in the waters off North Carolina. Fortunately for the Spanish diver, it turned out to be a nonfatal unprovoked attack.

June 1894
Craven County, Species Uncertain

Details about this attack in the waters of the Neuse off New Bern are very sketchy. So far, the only account of this incident is from an eyewitness who saw a soldier lose a foot to a shark. The unidentified writer (anonymous, 1894) noted, "At Newbern, N.C., I saw a soldier seized by a shark while in bathing. The shark seized the right leg just below the knee and stripped the flesh off clean to the ankle, but not further. The point of a tooth was found on the bone. He might perhaps have unjointed the leg at the knee, but he could not have snapped it off."

Exactly when this incident took place is unknown, which makes it difficult to learn any further details of this attack. If the incident took place in the summer, the most likely suspect would be a bull shark.

September 1895
Brunswick County, Species Uncertain

Sharks such as the shortfin mako, *Isurus oxyrinchus*, are known to, on occasion, leap into the open cockpit of fishing boats on the high seas. Other species ram boats, especially if they are threatened or tormented in some way. One incident of a shark (not a mako) ramming a boat—more in self-defense than in pursuit of prey—occurred off Southport in September 1895. As the story goes, Robert Ruark, Hoyle Dosher and Elmer Adkins left Southport in an open boat to go fishing near the mouth of the Cape Fear River off Fort Caswell. Dosher hooked a shark they estimated to be five feet long. The shark did not appreciate being hooked, and in an effort to free itself, it charged the boat. When the fish struck their small craft, Ruark was knocked overboard and landed "a-straddle the shark's back." Taking advantage of the ensuing confusion, the shark broke free and made a dive for deeper water with Ruark still clinging to its back.

Ruark rescued himself from a sure drowning—if not from being the dinner for this shark—by grabbing the fishing pole that Dosher had extended out toward him. After the victim grabbed hold of the pole, Dosher and Adkins pulled their companion back into the boat.

7

SHARK ATTACKS OF THE EARLY TWENTIETH CENTURY

The first decades of the twentieth century saw an increase in the number of people using the coast for a variety of reasons. News of the diverse shark fauna inhabiting local waters drew many commercial fishermen to the area to help harvest the bounty. But in addition to these operations taking large numbers of sharks, tourists were drawn to area beaches in search of fun in the sun. Thus, it is no surprise that negative encounters between humans and sharks occurred more frequently.

1903
Carteret County, Great White Shark/
Carcharodon carcharias

Dr. Russell Coles was, without question, the most notable shark researcher of his day. The retired tobacco farmer from Danville, Virginia, spent his summers along the southern Outer Banks, documenting the marine fauna he found and providing a glimpse into what was a fast-changing marine ecosystem. The reports he wrote of his exploits while fishing for the elasmobranch fauna of the area near Cape Lookout piqued the interest of President Theodore Roosevelt, who made a trip to Florida with Coles and his crew to hunt for manta rays. The two men became fast friends, but Roosevelt died before he could join Coles for a shark fishing trip off Shackleford Banks.

President Teddy Roosevelt died before he got the chance to fish for sharks and manta rays with his friend Russell Coles off Cape Lookout. They are shown here in March 1917, "dressed for devil-fishing" off Captiva Island, Florida, where Coles assembled a team from Carteret County on short notice to help the former president hunt giant manta rays. *Photograph courtesy of the Library of Congress.*

Coles was an advocate for exploiting sharks as a renewable resource of food and hides, setting up a commercial shark fishing operation at Cape Lookout. Others were already in operation in Morehead City, but it was Coles who took the time to document many of the animals they caught, sending notes to publications in New York and Washington, D.C. He also packed up some of the samples of the sharks and other marine life he caught for museums across the country.

Coles led an adventurous life. Often armed with a harpoon and a long knife, he prowled the waters near Cape Lookout and the Shackleford Banks on his quest for sharks. On numerous occasions, his fishing trips turned dangerous. One incident took place in 1903 in the Cape Lookout Bight. He was out harpooning turtles when a great white estimated to be eighteen feet long made several threatening moves toward his small skiff. Armed on this occasion with a big knife, a harpoon and a high-powered rifle, Coles watched warily as the huge shark sized up his small boat. The great white retreated about one hundred yards before turning and making what Coles was sure was its final charge in for the kill. But before the shark could reach its prey, it veered off at the last second and took a loggerhead turtle instead.

Coles later said of the incident, "I am convinced that this shark had satisfied himself that I was suitable food and had only retired to acquire speed for leaping into the skiff and seizing me, and that the coming to the surface of the turtle at that instant was all that saved me from a dangerous knife and shagreen fight." We unfortunately have few detailed accounts of such encounters as this one, in which a wily shark turned the tables on Coles, no doubt due to the fact that, to him, it was just an acceptable risk associated with his dangerous passion.

Summer 1905
Cartert County, Two Uncertain,
One Great White/*Carcharodon carcharias*

The year 1905 was one in which there were multiple shark attacks documented in the waters of North Carolina. We are fortunate that some details were chronicled briefly in the press about these incidents, but some stories were quashed by nervous tourism promoters. These promoters did such a thorough job in cleaning up the area's reputation for shark attacks that it is almost impossible to piece together what occurred, especially to one pound-net fisherman at Ocracoke.

Two years after Coles had his run-in with the great white at Cape Lookout, a similar nearly tragic episode occurred, this one with a great white measuring an estimated twenty feet long. As with Coles's earlier adventure, the timely arrival of a loggerhead turtle captured the shark's attention and ended the encounter before anyone got hurt (except the turtle, of course). The next day, Coles harpooned this turtle and found teeth marks thirty inches wide left behind by the shark. The shark managed to tear away the hapless loggerhead's right rear flipper and a part of its shell.

In July 1905, one particularly brutal shark attack that proved fatal took place in the inshore waters of Core Sound, near the Down East community of Davis Shore in Carteret County. Sutton Davis, a sixteen-year-old boy, was wading in chest-deep water, apparently playing with friends and not fishing or pulling nets. A press account (anonymous, 1905) of the incident noted:

> *Young Davis was in the water about waist deep, when suddenly, a shark approached him, threw him in the air, caught him as he struck the water, pulled him under and disappeared in the deep water with the boy. Thorough search has been made, but no particle of his body has been found. Those that were with the boy were terribly frightened and could not help him. The occurrence has thrown a feeling of horror over our town. The citizens and the guests of the community, particularly the children, have enjoyed the fine dives and invigorating swimming matches which they daily participate in.*

The account went on to point out that several sharks had been seen in local waters, drawn there by the bloody fish refuse being discarded into nearby waters by the local fishermen, who were cleaning large numbers of fish taken during what had proven to be a successful fishing season.

This attack was probably the handiwork of a great white or a bull shark, though a tiger shark cannot be totally ruled out. Tiger sharks generally move north from Florida as the waters warm in summer and are drawn west in the vicinity of Cape Lookout thanks to the natural gyre formed by currents branching off from the Gulf Stream and circulating off Shackleford and Bogue Banks all the way to Beaufort Inlet. Tiger sharks, which generally inhabit warmer waters, follow these warm currents as they feed, slowly moving up the coast. Noted for their cosmopolitan and voracious appetites, tiger sharks could easily have been lured into Core Sound thanks to the large amount of blood that was reported to have been accumulating over the preceding days, so they cannot be totally ruled out.

At roughly the same time as the deadly shark attack in Davis, there were two other shark fatalities in North Carolina waters. Both occurred just across Pamlico Sound at Ocracoke. Schwartz (2003) chronicled the two additional fatalities, one of which occurred sometime between 1900 and 1905 and the other of which occurred in 1905. Both of these deaths were corroborated by individuals who were interviewed by C. Felix Harvey, who was gathering data for early twentieth-century shark fatalities off Ocracoke for the U.S. Navy, in 1945.

Some might contend that the attacks at Ocracoke and Davis Shore were the works of some sort of rogue man-eating shark. Its appetite for human flesh stimulated by its feast at Davis Shore, the shark may have decided to feed on some hapless pound-net fisherman as it headed back out to sea via Ocracoke Inlet. However, more needs to be known about the timing and nature of the attacks at Ocracoke before any such theories can be proven.

JULY 1916
CARTERET COUNTY, SPECIES UNCERTAIN

On July 29, 1916, William Nelson was bitten by a shark while tending to his fishing nets near the Carteret County town of Atlantic. We know few details of the incident, with one press report (anonymous, 1916) giving brief mention: "William Nelson of Atlantic, while fishing with a haul net in the waters of Core Sound, caught a good-sized shark in the net by the tail fin and tried to get the big fish clear of the net. He became entangled in it and

A group of recreational fishermen along Shackleford Banks with what appears to be a sandbar shark circa 1910. *Photograph courtesy of North Carolina Archives and History.*

fell, and as soon as he loosened his hold, the shark caught his right arm in his mouth. From last reports, there are grave fears that Nelson will lose the injured member." There is no record of whether Nelson lost his arm due to the attack or recovered.

What is significant about Nelson's encounter with the shark is that it occurred at the same time as more famous shark attacks were playing out up the coast along Matawan Creek and other locations on the New Jersey shore. People were very nervous about shark activity that summer thanks to the attacks in New Jersey, where five youths were attacked (four fatally) during a series of shark attacks that occurred over a two-week period. There was a heightened awareness of sharks, with many reports that sharks were seen in larger numbers along the North Carolina coast than was usual. There were also attempts by many people, especially those with interests in the tourist business along the coast, to show that incidents such as these were aberrations and that it was safe to head to the beach.

SUMMER 1918
CARTERET COUNTY, GREAT WHITE SHARK/
CARCHARODON CARCHARIAS

Nearly a decade after his earlier encounter, Coles had another dangerous run-in with a great white in the Cape Lookout Bight. This was by far his most perilous adventure, and it nearly ended in the shark hunter's demise. After trying to lure in a great white he spotted into shallow water along the beach, Coles jumped out of his boat and pushed the small craft about one hundred yards away from where he was standing. Secured to his boat with a rope, armed with a harpoon and wading in five feet of water, he decided to tempt the great white shark even further by throwing pieces of crushed-up fish into the water.

The shark, which until then had paid scant attention to Coles, could no longer resist the human's dinner invitation. From a half mile away, the scent of the fish remains drew the shark literally into Coles's grasp. Moving with unexpected speed, the great white charged Coles from about one hundred feet away.

The redoubtable Coles was ready, and he met the charging great white with a blow from his harpoon. He described what happened next:

I met the onrushing shark by hurling my harpoon clear to the socket into it, near the angle of the jaw, and as the iron entered its flesh, the shark leaped forward, catching me in the angle formed by its head and the harpoon handle, which caught me just under the right arm, bruising me badly, while my face and neck were somewhat lacerated by coming in contact with the rough hide of the side of its head. As my right arm was free, it was a great chance for using the heavy knife, with which I was armed, had my tackle been strong; but the force of the blow snapped the poorly made harpoon at the socket, and the shark escaped, although it carried its death wound. I never again employed the same blacksmith to forge my harpoons, but that poorly made iron surely brought to a sudden ending a most exciting situation.

History and marine science owe quite a debt to this hapless blacksmith from Morehead City, for it is certain that had the poorly constructed harpoon not broken and allowed the great white to escape, Coles would not have survived the encounter and would not have lived to publish his captivating and educational accounts of his adventures with the large sharks off Cape Lookout.

September 1935
Onslow County, Bull Shark / *Carcharhinus leucas*

On September 21, 1935, Jere Fountain, Jim Collins and Collins's father-in-law, Paul Venters, all of Onslow County, were camping on an island overlooking Bear Inlet between Onslow Beach and Bear Island in what is now part of the Camp Lejeune Marine Corps Base. Around 8:30 p.m., after an arduous trip requiring not only rowing across the Intracoastal Waterway but also a bit of bushwhacking through thick woods to reach the spot where they would spend the next couple of days relaxing, the men decided to go swimming in the waters of Brown's Inlet.

"My father loved to swim," recalled Fountain's daughter, Frances Fountain Shaw, who, years later, penned an account of the tragic events that transpired that September night in 1935 with the help of her mother, Annie Cavanaugh Fountain, "and I can remember watching him floating far out on the waves while smoking his pipe. We used to spend a week almost every summer at this same beach while I was growing up. The house was a very rustic and primitive one with no inside plumbing, electricity or telephone. Mother didn't want Daddy to go away that weekend (she was afraid of the water), but he told her that it would probably be the last chance they would have to go that summer, and it was."

Brown's Inlet was known as a good place for catching drum, as evidenced by this photograph of an unidentified boy with a "prize drum" taken at Brown's Inlet in Onslow County in 1932. *An H.H. Brimley photograph courtesy of North Carolina Archives and History.*

As they were wading in waist-deep water, Fountain called out to his companions, standing roughly ten feet away, for help, as something big had bitten him. His companions quickly made their way to their wounded friend, keeping a wary eye out for any fins cutting through the surface of the water in case the animal returned to finish off its stricken prey. They made their way through the surf unmolested as they dragged their wounded friend up onto the beach. Fountain soon passed out as his

Fishermen at Brown's Inlet, where Jere Fountain was killed by a bull shark in September 1935, circa 1930. *An H.H. Brimley photograph courtesy of North Carolina Archives and History.*

friends tried to stem the flow of blood pouring from the wound with pieces of their clothing torn into makeshift tourniquets. Try as they might, neither Venters nor Collins were able to stop the flow of blood coming from the grievous wound just above Fountain's knee.

There were, of course, no telephones or lifeguard stands on this remote stretch of coast, but they knew their friend needed immediate medical attention if he was to survive. So, they decided that the younger Collins would make the dash through the woods to see if he could track down a doctor.

> *Jim Collins rushed for the boat and Daddy's car to go for help and left his father-in-law on the beach with him. In his haste and excitement, Jim ran into a tree and wrecked the car. He then thumbed a ride with a man in a pickup truck. He told the driver to move over and let him drive because he had to get to Jacksonville to a doctor fast. It was several hours before Jim and Dr. John Henderson arrived back at the beach, only to learn that my father had died within minutes after Jim had left. The doctor said that the main artery in Jere's leg had been severed and that he had bled to death.*

Jere Fountain quickly bled to death there on the sandy beach overlooking Brown's Inlet, and it is unlikely he would have lived, even if trained rescue paramedics were nearby to treat his wounds. It took quite an effort to bring

Recreational anglers at Brown's Inlet circa 1932. *An H.H. Brimley photograph courtesy of North Carolina Archives and History.*

Shark attack victim Jere Fountain rests with his wife, Annie, in a family cemetery in rural Onslow County.

his body back from the beach to the nearest funeral home in Jacksonville. His daughter recalled, "It was hours later before the doctor and Daddy's friends were able to get his body across the waterway in the boat and to the funeral home in Jacksonville. At four o'clock Sunday morning, Jim Collins, Dr. Henderson, and my mother's sister, Hazel Mizelle, arrived at our house with the terrible news. It was the saddest day of our lives and one we will never forget."

Fountain was a rural mail carrier in Richlands who left behind his young wife and their three children. The *New Bern Tribune* (1935) later wrote of Fountain's wounds, "The leg was nearly severed above the knee. Coroner Kimmon Jones stated he was certain that prints of a shark's teeth were on Fountain's body." Such detailed information made it clear that this was the handiwork of a shark.

We are fortunate that Fountain's widow and daughter took the time to chronicle the events that transpired on the Onslow County beach, as it helps remind us that such tragedies do not happen within a vacuum but often affect an extended network of people far beyond just the victim and their immediate family.

The location of the attack near the mouth of an inlet, the time of year and the depth of the water point strongly to a bull shark as the most likely culprit. However, bull sharks have generally started moving south to warmer waters by this time of year, so there is a small chance that new evidence may come to light that points to a great white shark as the species responsible.

May 1936
Carteret County, Species Uncertain

On May 26, 1936, Colonel J.W. Baker and his family were vacationing at their family cottage near Cape Lookout when Baker was bitten on the foot by a shark. First aid was rendered at the U.S. Coast Guard station before he was transported to Morehead City for further treatment at the hospital. Baker was an official with the Blue Bell Overall Company of Greensboro. No details of this particular shark are recorded (anonymous, 1936).

August 1936
Dare County, Bull Shark/*Carcharhinus leucas*

Fishermen who worked the shallow waters of the sounds and estuaries along the North Carolina coast had frequent contact with sharks and looked on them as an occupational hazard as well as competitor for the same fish stocks. Most scrapes with sharks were not really considered newsworthy, unless there was serious injury or loss of life. Thus, accounts of encounters with sharks and fishermen were seldom chronicled. For that reason, we are fortunate that details of two teenagers fishing near Frisco in August 1936 did not go undocumented.

James Mitchell-Hedges and his friend Raymond McHenry were in a rowboat roughly one hundred yards offshore in the waters of Pamlico Sound, checking the fishing nets they had set the previous evening. They were wading in the waist-deep water north of Hatteras Island, removing fish from their net and, in the process, spilling bloody fish remains into the water. All of these gory fish acted like a big ball of chum, which divers use today to draw the attention of sharks in nearby waters for the benefit of tourists in places like Australia and South Africa. Soon, one of the boys noticed they had attracted the attention of a large shark swimming nearby, as its fin was cutting through the water, heading straight for them. They managed to hop into their rowboat just as the shark streaked by, splashing water from its tail into their craft. The frustrated shark was not finished, as it managed to grab the bow of the boat in its mouth, hoping to shake the occupants into the water, but to no avail.

All this activity in the water had attracted more sharks to the scene, no doubt looking for what promised to be a good meal. The boys counted at least ten more shark fins circling their boat, getting ever closer to their prey. But one of the larger sharks got entangled in the boys' net, so they took the opportunity to row with all their speed for shore, towing the large shark behind. They counted a dozen sharks following them before they managed to reach shore with their damaged boat.

According to a press account (anonymous, 1936), "The captured fish measured 11 feet in length and weighed approximately 700 pounds. The jaws were four feet, seven inches in circumference." Such aggressive behaviour in the shallow inshore waters of Pamlico Sound point to a bull shark most likely being the boys' main antagonist, though some of the other smaller nearshore species may have been drawn to all the commotion as well as the blood trail.

November 1937
Carteret or Dare County,
Multiple Species Unknown

The wreck of the Greek freighter *Tzenny Chandris* on November 13, 1937, reminded the world that even as people made technological advances, there are still times when the powerful forces of nature will prevail, especially if one is careless in seeing to the fine details of making sure one's ship and crew are ready to deal with issues often encountered in dangerous places, such as the Outer Banks of North Carolina. The ship was overloaded with cargo, primarily scrap iron, so much so that it dragged ground while backing out from the dock at Morehead City.

The ship began taking on water almost as soon as it cleared Beaufort Inlet, and several of its more experienced crewmen advised turning back before something serious went wrong. But its young captain, George Couhopadelis, refused to listen to reason and stubbornly stuck to his course, even as the ship encountered heavy swells and freshening winds from an approaching storm. It didn't take long for the ship, already lying low in the water, to drop even lower thanks to water pouring into its hold. The men renewed their pleas to the captain to return to a safe harbor, but he remained obstinate until it was too late. The ship was taking in water too quickly for the pumps to clear it out, and the *Tzenny Chandris* foundered in the ocean somewhere between Hatteras and Cape Lookout.

The radio operator, hesitant to go against the captain's orders, sent out an SOS signal only after being forced at gunpoint by several of his shipmates. However, in his haste, the operator forgot to include the ship's position in the distress call, so the radio operators at the coast guard station in Fort Macon were unable to get a reliable pin on where the troubled ship was actually located.

The crewmen who managed to scramble to safety before the ship went down found no refuge in the lifeboat, which capsized and sank beneath the surface. The men were forced to supplement their life vests by clinging to whatever piece of floating debris they might have found in the water to help them remain afloat.

The tanker *Swiftsure* was heading northbound off Cape Lookout and was passing nearby at the time the *Tzenny Chandris* went down. The *Swiftsure*'s crew began looking about to see if they could find any signs of the troubled ship. After searching for about five hours, they found the first group of survivors

LIFE ON THE AMERICAN NEWSFRONT: GREEK FREIGHTER SINKS OFF CAPE HATTERAS

Bound for Rotterdam with a cargo of scrap iron, the Greek freighter *Tzenny Chandris* cleared Morehead City, N.C., on Nov. 11. Early next evening an autumn gale boiled up from the east, hurled dreadful seas over her stern, flooded her engine room, extinguished her lights. Forty miles off Cape Hatteras the *Tzenny Chandris* rolled over on her beam and sank.

Six crew members who had managed to launch a lifeboat were picked up after five hours by a northbound tanker. The other lifeboats capsized and for over 30 hours the captain and 14 sailors clung to bits of floating wreckage in shark-haunted waters till patrol planes sighted them and sent a Coast Guard cutter to their rescue. Of a crew of 28, seven were lost.

Rescued after 30 hours in the angry November sea, this sailor stretches out his arms to Coast Guardsmen of the cutter *Mendota*. With 14 others he had been plunged into the waves when their crowded lifeboat overturned in gale.

Captain Coufopandelis of *Tzenny Chandris* tells how a sailor went mad from drinking salt water, bit him on the nose.

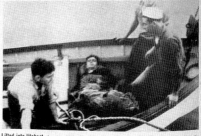

Helpless in the open sea, this aged seaman and his companions were forced constantly to thrash their arms and legs to frighten away sharks attracted by debris of the shipwreck.

Lifted into lifeboat of cutter *Mendota*, the sailors collapse from exhaustion. Coast Guardsmen were guided to shipwreck survivors by smoke bombs dropped from patrol planes.

Shivering and exhausted, the rescued sailors are rowed back to the *Mendota*. Four dead men also were taken from the ocean by Coast Guardsmen. Three others never were found.

The drowned and the delivered are borne ashore in baskets and stretchers on *Mendota's* arrival at Norfolk. At Boston six others, picked up by a tanker, were docked the same day.

The tragic story of the Greek freighter *Tzenny Chandris*, which went down in the "shark-haunted waters" off Hatteras in November 1937, made international news, gracing the pages of the November 29, 1937 edition of *Life* magazine.

not far from where the ship had sunk. But not all of the survivors were part of this group. Another group was whisked northeast by strong winds and the Gulf Stream.

Miraculously, these men were spotted almost one hundred miles off Kitty Hawk by naval aviator Lieutenant A.C. Keller, who contacted the coast guard, which immediately dispatched the cutter *Mendota* to rescue them. Keller dropped smoke bombs in the water to mark the position to aid the search and rescue teams operating nearby. One of the coast guard aircraft was piloted by Lieutenant Richard Burke.

After seeing several bodies floating in the water, he spied two men wearing life preservers violently kicking at something beneath the surface of the ocean, desperately fighting off something that was attacking them from below. "Everywhere you looked, there were sharks," Burke reported shortly after the incident (anonymous, 1937). "We immediately dropped smoke bombs and zoomed about over the men to call the attention of the *Mendota* to their location. We had about decided to take a chance and land in an attempt to rescue the men when the *Mendota* put over a small boat and took them aboard."

Commander Henry Coyle, the master of the *Mendota*, could hardly believe the stories he was hearing about the *Tzenny Chandris*'s crewmen's battle with the sharks. One of the men told of watching helplessly as one of his mates was pulled bodily through his lifebelt into the ocean below by a ravenous shark (anonymous, 1937).

The *Tzenny Chandris* brought international attention to the North Carolina coast. The sad story of the plight of the survivors of the ill-fated ship made it into the pages of *Life* magazine (1937), which referred to the waters off the Outer Banks as "those shark-haunted waters."

May 1939
Carteret County, Multiple Species Unknown

On May 6, 1939, the British freighter *Hunliffe* was nearing the end of its run from Galveston, Texas, to Newport News, Virginia, when it was hit by a rogue wave, which swept one of its crewmen, James Heagan, overboard into the sea over one hundred miles southeast of Cape Henry. The captain of the vessel ordered it to immediately turn about to pick up the sailor. However, before he could be rescued, Heagan was eaten by sharks while the *Hunliffe*'s terrified crewmen looked on in terror.

A press account (anonymous, 1939) noted, "Heagan was a powerful swimmer, his mates said, and was making good progress toward the ship as she hove to. A lifebuoy was tossed out, and as he headed toward it, the men prepared to lower a lifeboat. Then they saw sharks....A few minutes later, Heagan cried out, threw up his arms and sank as if jerked."

No descriptions of the sharks were given, nor any mention of theories of the species responsible. The offshore waters on the edge of the Gulf Stream are a prime habitat for oceanic whitetips, makos and blue sharks, as well as hammerheads.

July 1940
Brunswick County, Tiger Shark/*Galeocerdo cuvier*

On July 1, 1940, William Dye of Charlotte was vacationing with his family at Holden Beach when he decided to do some fishing in the surf. After Dye landed a fish, which he secured to a stringer tied about his waist and left dangling in the waist-deep water, a large shark decided to relieve him of his catch and moved in for the kill. Witnesses (anonymous, 1940) claimed, "The shark, reported by some to have been about 10 feet long, presumably attempted to grab the fish from the belt and took a chunk out of Dye's leg between the knee and the hip in slashing by." This is clearly what the International Shark Attack File would categorize as a provoked shark attack.

No one left a description of the shark, aside from its length. This was probably the work of a tiger shark, which frequent this stretch of coast in the summer months. As mentioned earlier, some record tiger sharks have been taken in the waters of Brunswick County between Southport and Myrtle Beach.

A tiger shark has the distinction of being the largest fish ever caught from a fishing pier along the Carolina coast. Walter Maxwell of Charlotte, North Carolina, was fishing from the Cherry Grove Pier just across the border in South Carolina on June 14, 1964, when, after a gruelling five-hour battle, he landed a tiger shark of enormous propensities. There were no scales in this rural coastal town large enough to accurately weigh this monstrous fish. So, the next day, the shark was placed on a truck and driven to the nearby town of Loris, where an adequate set of scales was found. Maxwell's tiger shark weighed 1,780 pounds, a world record. Witnesses aver that had the shark been weighed right after it was taken and not allowed to dry out on the beach for a day, the weight would have been even higher.

There has been some confusion regarding the length of Maxwell's record-breaking shark, with the size of the shark reported as being more than twenty feet long. In his book *Shark Safari*, shark researcher Hal Scharp (1975) gave the following details about the shark caught on June 14, 1964: "Maxwell's I.G.F.A. all-tackle record shark weighed 1,780 pounds, measured 13 feet, 10½ inches long, and had a girth of 103 inches. He caught this brute in 1964 from a pier at Cherry Grove, South Carolina. His catch eclipsed the old record of 1,432 pounds caught in 1958 off Cape Moreton, Australia."

Maxwell's record stood for nearly forty years before it was eclipsed by an Australian fisherman. According to the International Game Fish Association, the record was broken by Kevin Clapson of Ulladulla, New South Wales, Australia, who landed a 1,785.11-pound tiger shark on March 28, 2004.

Scharp (1975) recorded the details of another memorable shark that Maxwell encountered while fishing for tiger sharks off Brunswick County.

> On another occasion, while battling with a 1,200-pound tiger, Maxwell spotted the largest shark he had ever seen. The giant zeroed in on Maxwell's hooked tiger, attacked (taking a large chunk out of it) and then disappeared. Maxwell brought his tiger in and examined the huge, gaping wound, measuring 36 inches across. Judging from its size and shape of the tooth marks, he estimated that the attack may have been made by a white shark that would have weighed at least 3,500 pounds!

Two years after landing his world-record tiger shark, Maxwell, a few miles up the coast, caught another record-breaking tiger shark. This one was taken off the Yaupon Beach Pier and weighed 1,150.8 pounds. This set an official record for a tiger shark caught in North Carolina that has never been eclipsed. Thus, Maxwell has the distinction of holding the record for the largest tiger sharks taken in both North and South Carolina.

December 1943
Carteret County, Multiple Species Unknown

The waters off North Carolina became even more menacing than usual for mariners after the outbreak of World War II, when German U-boats began operations off the coast of the United States in January 1942. German U-boats sank over four hundred Allied ships, both warships and civilian freighters carrying valuable cargo needed for the Allied war effort in Europe, in the Graveyard of the Atlantic. The stretch of sea between Cape Lookout and Cape Hatteras formed a natural bottleneck, where shipping was constricted due to several factors. This area became known as Torpedo Alley or Torpedo Junction, as German commanders found the slow-moving ships particularly inviting targets. Most official estimates place the death toll of Torpedo Alley at over five thousand over the course of the war off North Carolina.

Many of the casualties were killed outright but not all. It is of great credit to both the coast guard and the navy that so many people from both sides

CUBAN SEAMAN IS TREATED FOR SHARK BITE.

Julie Caba Rocas, here shown receiving treatment for shark bite from maritime service Pharmacist's Mate, 2/C C. H. Britt, of Raleigh, N. C., clung to a splintered hatch cover for 36 hours after the Cuban freighter Libertad was torpedoed and sunk. During the day and a half in the water 10 other members of the crew drowned, leaving as survivors Rocas, Rufino Nadal (left) and Melchur De León (shirtless.) Nadal was in the water 53 hours. Rocas was rescued by an American naval vessel.

Photographs of crewmen from the ill-fated *Libertad* receiving treatment for shark bites appeared in newspapers across the country, including the *Greensboro Record*.

survived these military encounters. The United States' investment in air-sea rescue during the war continues to pay dividends today.

We will never know exactly how many of the people who survived the initial assaults on their vessels subsequently lost their lives to sharks and other denizens of the deep while waiting for rescue. Stories of the ordeals of many of those who battled a different enemy after being plunged into shark-infested waters around the world led military leaders to redouble their research into ways to help mitigate such factors in future conflicts. Perhaps the best known of these were the survivors of the ill-fated USS *Indianapolis* in the Pacific.

Sharks remained some of the prime natural hazards to mariners who were plunged into the seas off North Carolina during World War II, a fact best demonstrated by the misadventures of the crew of a Cuban freighter that was sunk by a German U-boat off Cape Lookout just before Christmas 1943. The *U-129*, under the command of Kapitanleutnant Richard von Harpe, sank the freighter *Libertad* by putting four torpedoes into it after it rounded Cape Lookout heading north on December 4, 1943. Though some have erroneously claimed the *Libertad* was sunk off Charleston, South Carolina, the attack occurred at 34°12'N, 75°20'W, which is several miles offshore between Hatteras and Cape Lookout, along the coast of North Carolina. Even though the *Libertad* was part of a convoy of ships that had been organized to reduce hazards from U-boats operating in the area, it sank beneath the waves, unnoticed by the other members of the convoy, which sped north toward Virginia.

Almost two days passed before the crew of the *Libertad* were finally hauled out of the waters of the Atlantic to safety. Only eighteen of the forty-three crew members survived, and many of them were rescued by aircraft and an assortment of ships aided by blimps from the base at Weeksville. Julio Cabarracas, Rufino Nadal and Melchur de Leon were among the survivors of the attack. Rocas and De Leon spent over fifty hours in the sea, clinging desperately to a splintered hatch cover and fighting off sharks.

Press reports of the attack (anonymous, 1943) noted, "Cabarracas said that before the blimp dropped the raft, he and De Leon were surrounded by sharks, 'We fought them off with our hands and our feet. After a while, I got tired, and at that moment, a shark bit me on my side.' Naval physicians who treated Cabarracas said the wound bore teeth marks." Rocas spent an agonising fifty-three hours in the water before finally being rescued.

Other reports state that at least ten members of Rocas's fellow crewmen from the *Libertad* were victims of the sharks that arrived in large numbers shortly after the ship went down and continued harassing survivors until the hapless men were pulled from the waters. One report (anonymous, 1943) stated, "Eighteen survivors clung to overturned boats and a splintered hatch-cover for 53 hours, while ten others became exhausted, dropped off, and were seized by sharks." A photograph of Rocas that was taken while he was in the infirmary shows he was being treated by Pharmacists' Mate Second Class C.H. Britt of Raleigh, North Carolina, for shark bites.

The survivors of the *Libertad* never provided any details about exactly which species of sharks were causing them the most trouble. No doubt, this veritable human smorgasbord drew a variety of the pelagic species to feast, especially oceanic whitetips and blue sharks.

August 1945
Hyde County, Species Unknown

The final resting place of John Kuenstier, who was killed by a shark at Ocracoke on August 16, 1945, in the New Bern National Cemetery. At the time of his death, Kuenstier and his fellow crewmen were celebrating President Truman's announcement of the surrender of the Empire of Japan, ending World War II.

One of the most enigmatic fatal shark attacks along the coast of North Carolina took place along the Outer Banks during the waning days of World War II. Information about the attack remains hard to come by due to several factors, including wartime censorship that was still in place when the attack took place, as well as the secret nature of the military unit to which the victim was assigned.

What we do know is that the attack occurred in the surf near the airport that now stands on Ocracoke Island. On August 16, 1945, several men from the beach jumper units who were training at the Amphibious Training Base Ocracoke were relaxing, as the enlisted men had been given a field day on the beach to celebrate news of the surrender of the Empire of Japan. One of these men was John Edward Kuenstier, a man about whom little has been recorded. His grave marker at the National Cemetery in New Bern mentions that the twenty-two-year-old sailor hailed from New York, held the rank of electricians' mate third class and was assigned to BJU-7, or Beach Jumper Unit 7, which was part of a unit made up of commandos and special operations personnel who were headquartered at ATB Ocracoke.

Details about exactly what happened that day are not well known, as official naval records give scant information about the incident. But C. Felix Harvey of Kinston, North Carolina, was one of the naval officers present at the outing and personally witnessed the vicious shark attack.

Kuenstier decided to take a swim in the late afternoon. "He swam out past the breakers a good ways, about fifty yards," recalled Harvey.

> *Next thing we knew, we heard him yelling and screaming. At first, we thought he was having a heart attack or something. But then we saw a trail of blood on the water and knew it was a shark. We managed to get him back on the beach, but he died right there before the ambulance could take him to the infirmary. The shark had bitten him twice. The first time, it hit him on the lower part of his leg, but you could see where its teeth had been deflected by the bone. Then it took another bite, this one in the large muscle of the thigh. The bite mark was thirteen inches wide, and it nearly took his leg off.*

Afterward, Harvey was instructed by Captain Anthony Rorshach to compile a report on the incident. Unfortunately, the report Harvey so diligently prepared and submitted to his captain has been lost through the years. But Harvey recalled that his extensive interviews with several local people turned up some intriguing facts about not only the 1945 incident but also previous fatal shark attacks that had taken place in the waters off Ocracoke.

> *I spoke with several of the older folks, and they told me this was not the first time a shark had killed somebody at Ocracoke. I documented two cases in particular that stood out to me, one from 1900 and another from 1905. In both cases, the victims were drum fishermen who were wearing waders as they fished in the water there at the tip of Ocracoke, where it meets Ocracoke Inlet.*

There has been much speculation about which specific species of shark was responsible for the attack on Kuenstier. There is a persistent and long-lived rumor that this was the handiwork of a great white shark, but Harvey maintained that he was unable to document such details about the shark itself, as Kuenstier died on the beach before he could provide any clues about the shark's identity. To his knowledge, there were neither detailed studies made of the wounds, nor fragments of teeth preserved that could later provide further illumination about the specific species involved.

Several of the sailors spent many hours attempting to rid the waters near where the attack had taken place of any other potentially dangerous sharks that might still be lurking below. Harvey recalled:

> *We felt at the time that we actually caught the shark that was responsible for this attack just a short time afterwards. We fished that area pretty good, and one of us brought in a shark that was ten feet long, and when we measured its mouth, it was the same size as the bite in the sailor's leg, which was thirteen inches wide. So, several of us were satisfied that we had caught the shark. We didn't know exactly which species it was. Could have been a great white, I don't know for sure. But I do know it was not a hammerhead.*

Thus, the debate about whether this was the handiwork of a bull shark, great white or one of the other larger species of sharks found in these waters continues. There were several local leaders who thought it was a great white, and they went to great lengths to make sure details about the attack did not spread far. Perhaps in the future, Harvey's report that he compiled while the incident was fresh in people's minds will come to light and shed important information about this and other fatal shark attacks off the North Carolina Outer Banks during the first half of the twentieth century.

Kuenstier's remains were taken to New Bern and interred in the Federal Cemetery, where they rest today. He was one of the last servicemen to die serving their country along the North Carolina coast during World War II.

September 1947
Onslow County, Species Unknown

On September 10, 1947, Robert Sannino, an off-duty lifeguard at Onslow Beach on the Camp Lejeune Marine Corps Base in Pender County, was bitten while trying to relax while swimming in the waters just off the beach. Press reports (anonymous, 1947) note, "Pfc. Robert Sannino of Ocean City, N.J., went for a dip in his off-duty hours at Onslow Beach, a Marine

The salt marsh near New River Inlet attracts both lemon and bull sharks during the warm summer months.

recreation area. A shark ripped his right leg." There are too few details recorded to figure out which species was responsible for the bite.

Onslow Beach was much less secluded after World War II than it had been a dozen years earlier, when Fountain bled to death just north of this location as the result of an attack by a bull shark. Whether the early leadership at the base gained their knowledge of the dangers of sharks from quizzing locals or through trial and error is unknown.

8

LATE TWENTIETH-CENTURY SHARK ATTACKS

The latter half of the twentieth century saw many technological innovations as a result of World War II and the subsequent Cold War with the Soviet Union. Thanks to advances in communications, transportation, engineering and medicine, people pushed into environments where they never imagined going—the most memorable being space and the deep sea.

An exploding population along the coast brought more and more people into the waters where sharks had been hunting for millennia. However, the number of fatal shark attacks did not go up proportionally, as so many of the larger species of sharks had been culled from local waters. But the waters off North Carolina were not totally safe—not by a long shot.

July 1957
Carteret County, Great White Shark/
Carcharodon carcharias

One of the best-documented fatal unprovoked great white shark attacks of the twentieth century along the East Coast of the United States occurred in North Carolina on July 15, 1957, in the waters off Atlantic Beach in Carteret County, not far from Fort Macon, where, over the years, several fatal shark attacks have been documented. Unfortunately, the victim, Rupert Wade, shared the fate of these earlier victims and did not survive the ordeal.

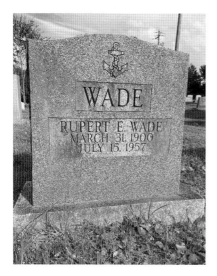

The grave of Rupert Wade in the Bayview Cemetery in Morehead City. A renowned long-distance swimmer, Wade was killed by a great white shark while swimming off Atlantic Beach, North Carolina, in July 1957.

A fifty-seven-year-old resident of Morehead City, Wade was a renowned long-distance swimmer who often amazed tourists at the local beaches with his swimming stamina. On this particular occasion, he was over one thousand feet offshore, swimming with a lifeguard named Billy Shaw. After about fifteen minutes in the water, Wade yelled out to his companion that a shark had bitten him. He told Shaw to swim for shore to get help, which his friend promptly did with all the speed he could muster.

The coast guard was immediately summoned from Fort Macon. When they arrived, coast guard crewmen spotted Wade floating on the water. Alive but unconscious, Wade was lifted into the boat and taken to the coast guard station where an ambulance was waiting. Despite the fact that they administered artificial respiration on the trip back, they were unable to revive Wade, who was pronounced dead at the Morehead City Hospital. He had bled to death as a result of the wounds inflicted by the shark.

The death of Wade was attributed a great white shark. He was bitten on the right leg midway between his hip and knee, ripping deep enough into his flesh to expose the bone in his leg. He also had several deep cuts on his right foot.

Wade was the last confirmed great white shark fatality on the coast of North Carolina, at least at the time of this book's publication.

Circa 1960

County Unknown, Thresher Shark/*Alopias vulpinas*

There is a persistent story frequently told among shark enthusiasts that a thresher shark was responsible for a fatal attack on a human off the Outer Banks of North Carolina. This particular bit of lore appears to have

Shark hunter Frank Mundus reported that a thresher shark, like this one, which he caught off the coast of New York in 1978, decapitated an unlucky fisherman off the coast of North Carolina several years earlier. *Photograph courtesy of the Library of Congress.*

originated with shark fisherman Frank Mundus, who was famed for his exploits in catching sharks off Montauk, New York, in the mid-twentieth century. Mundus wrote a book, *Sportfishing for Sharks*, which included a chapter on thresher sharks. The following is his account of the affair:

> *A grisly story underscores the claim. Down off the Carolinas, two men were commercial shark fishing with longlines. They were servicing their lines one day when the boat's winch slowed under the strain of a fairly large shark. As the beast was lifted to the surface, one of the men leaned over the gunnel to see what it was. The catch turned out to be a huge thresher, perhaps 16 feet long overall. As the man leaned outboard, the thresher swung his powerful tail. Its tip section caught the fisherman in the neck and cut off his head with the dispatch of a guillotine. The severed head fell into the water and couldn't be recovered. His decapitated body dropped back into the cockpit. That gruesome accident happened to the father of a New Jersey school chum of ours.*

No other corroboration of this tragic episode has come to light yet, and no details, such as the victim's name or the date and exact location of the incident, have been preserved. The incident is included here in case someone has a bit more information about the episode. They are encouraged to turn over details to the International Shark Attack File or some such group that documents such incidents.

With their long, scythe-like tails, thresher sharks are some of the most easily recognised sharks in the ocean. Of the three species of thresher sharks that live in the world, two are found in the waters off the North Carolina coast—the common thresher, *Alopias vulpinas*, and the bigeye thresher, *Alopias superciliosus*. The latter lives in deep water and is seldom seen closer than seven miles offshore. But the common thresher is a regular visitor to North Carolina's shores.

They are sometimes commonly referred to as fox sharks or whiptail sharks, and tales abound of the threshers' ability to corral and capture prey utilizing their distinctive tails. Unless a person has seen one of these sharks in real life or has seen actual photographs of one of these fish, one might be tempted to believe that accounts of their herding and hunting prowess were based more on folklore than fact. Indeed, many of the stories may have been embellished through the years. But enough of these sharks' antics has been witnessed and chronicled by experts and eyewitnesses to prove that the thresher shark is no hoop snake of the seas. Thresher sharks were also known as strike-tail sharks

A common thresher shark landed along the coast of the Outer Banks. They are also known locally as whiptail sharks, thanks to the length of their tails in relation to the rest of their bodies. Did a shark such as this one use its tail to decapitate a fisherman off the North Carolina coast? *Ray Couch photograph, courtesy of the Outer Banks History Center.*

along the Carolina coast in the nineteenth century. An early correspondent from Fort Macon noted, "A strike-tail shark, the first we have ever seen, was brought over from the fort yesterday. His tail was just the length of head and body combined and seems to be his weapon of defence. The extreme length was nine feet."

The following is how Allen (1996) described the thresher shark's antics:

> *The thresher pursues schools of mackerel, bluefish, shad, menhaden, bonito, and various herrings. When it nears a school of fish, it splashes the water with its tail, driving the fish into a close-packed crowd and making smaller and smaller circles around them. Then, when the fish are jammed together in a frightened mass, the thresher darts among them, mouth agape, and swallows them. Sometimes, threshers, working as a team, herd the fish between them and, at the moment of slaughter, share the meal.*

A bigeye thresher shark caught on November 7, 1928, a mile off Wrightsville Beach. *Photograph courtesy of North Carolina Archives and History.*

Although they are not encountered as frequently along the North Carolina coast, bigeye threshers are seen in offshore waters during the cooler months of the year. On rare occasions, bigeye threshers have been encountered in nearshore waters. For instance, a bigeye thresher was caught a mile off Wrightsville Beach on November 7, 1928. Schwartz (2003) noted that a nearly ten-foot-long bigeye thresher was caught in the waters of Core Sound in May 1987.

Common threshers make their appearance in the fall along the Carolina coast. Dr. Schwartz pointed out that he has observed these large sharks coming close to shore along the Bogue Banks. "We see them in November as they come in right along the beach and go out past Swansboro, going south."

Common threshers were once quite prevalent along the shores of North Carolina, especially in the area around Cape Lookout. Russell Coles (1915) wrote that he had seen one in Cape Lookout Bight in July 1914. "Although I was very close to it, I did not have my harpoons at hand and could not capture it. At the time of observation, it was feeding in shallow water by throwing the fish to its mouth with its tail, and I saw one fish, which it failed to seize, thrown for a considerable distance, clear of the water."

Today, these sharks are becoming a rare sight and would seem to be facing a very bleak future. Researchers at Dalhousie University in Halifax, Nova Scotia, reported in 2003 that the population of threshers in the northwestern Atlantic Ocean had dropped by 80 percent since 1986. Thus, I feel fortunate to have stood on the beach at Fort Macon in 2015 when I witnessed a thresher shark working its way south, stunning fish in the surf and scattering some of its prey on the sand.

August 1976
Carteret County, Hammerhead/Specific
Subspecies Not Recorded

The earliest confirmed attack made by a hammerhead shark in the waters of North Carolina took place on August 25, 1976, in Carteret County. The exact subspecies involved was unfortunately not recorded. Randy Hall of High Point was bitten on the foot by a hammerhead while surfing near the Emerald Isle Pier. A press report (anonymous, 1976) noted that Hall did not believe the shark intended to attack him, and he said that the attack was a case of mistaken identity. "I think my foot was mistaken for a fish or something. There was a bite on it, and then I was released. I think it was an accident."

Hammerheads are regarded by researchers as one of the top ten most dangerous species of sharks in the world and have been known to attack humans. According to data compiled by researchers with the International Shark Attack File, the various species of hammerheads are tied for eighth place with spinner sharks at sixteen confirmed unprovoked attacks around the world through 2022. So far, no fatal hammerhead attacks have been confirmed in North Carolina waters.

With eyes fixed at the ends of their wing-like heads, hammerhead sharks look like some mythic beasts dreamed up by a science fiction writer's fertile imagination. But these creatures of the deep are very real and are frequent visitors to the shores of North Carolina.

Hammerheads make up a family of sharks known as the Sphyrnidae. There are ten known species that make up the family Sphyrnidae. These are the Carolina hammerhead, smooth hammerhead, small eye hammerhead, whitefin hammerhead, great hammerhead, bonnethead, scalloped hammerhead, winghead, scoophead and mallet head. Of the ten species of hammerheads, six are found in the waters of the Carolinas. These include the bonnethead, smooth hammerhead, scalloped hammerhead, Carolina hammerhead and great hammerhead. Three of these five species are known to attain large sizes in our waters.

Bonnethead sharks, *Sphyrna tiburo*, are the smallest members of the family Sphyrnidae found in the waters of North Carolina. They are distinguished by their heads, which are shaped more like a shovel than a hammer. They can grow up to five feet long.

Scalloped hammerheads, *Sphyrna lewini*, are found all along the North Carolina coast throughout much of the year. Schwartz (2003) noted that scalloped hammerheads can grow up to fourteen feet long. The largest scalloped hammerhead observed in the North Carolina was a little over ten feet long. He also recorded several specimens in nearshore waters and rivers, including the Cape Fear and North Rivers.

Carolina hammerheads, *Sphyrna gilberti*, are a newly identified species that researchers discovered living along the coast of the Palmetto State. They may eventually be found to inhabit other parts of the Atlantic, but for now, the only ones positively identified are off the coast of South Carolina. Researchers studied what they thought were eighty specimens of scalloped hammerheads caught off the South Carolina coast between 2001 and 2003. A detailed examination of genetic materials and a morphological examination revealed that fifty-four of the specimens were a distinct species of shark. Quatro and his collaborators (2013) observed, "*Sphyrna gilberti* sp. nov. can be distinguished from congeners by having a head length greater than 20% of STL, cephalofoil with median indentation, inner narial groove present, pelvic fins with straight rear margins, and 91 or fewer precaudal vertebrae." So far, no Carolina hammerheads have been documented in North Carolina waters, but it is only a matter of time before researchers identify one along the Brunswick County coast.

The smooth hammerhead, *Sphyrna zygena*, is found in the waters of North Carolina in the summer months. They can grow up to thirteen feet long. Many might be surprised to learn that the largest recorded smooth hammerhead from North Carolina was caught just off the waterfront of the port town of Beaufort in July 1906. The shark was harpooned as it circled a fishing boat anchored out in Taylor's Creek less than two hundred yards from shore. The shark was chasing a stingray when it was killed. The next day, E.W. Gudger of the U.S. Fisheries Laboratory in Beaufort obtained the shark. He studied the fish and made careful measurements of the remains. Gudger found the shark, which he classified as *Sphyrna zygena*, to be twelve feet, six inches long. The length of the hammer between the eyes was three feet. Perhaps most interesting is what he found inside the shark. Gudger (1947) noted, "When dissected, I found in the stomach an almost perfect skeleton of a stingray with many like fragments of other skeletons, and I got from its throat, mouth and jaws 54 stings, varying from perfect spines to broken-off tips—souvenirs of at least that many stingrays, caught and probably eaten. But for all these accumulated stings, this shark was a living dynamo of energy when harpooned."

Russell Coles and his team. Note the Cape Lookout Lighthouse in the background. *Photograph courtesy of the National Marine Fisheries Service.*

The great hammerhead, *Sphyrna mokarran*, is the largest of the various species of hammerhead sharks. Some that have been observed measured in excess of twenty feet long. Large specimens have been rarely caught, with the largest great hammerhead landed in recent years being caught off the coast of Australia in 2011.

The hammer of the great hammerhead is straighter than that of other hammerheads, forming more of a straight line across the front of its head, except for an indentation in the middle. Another distinguishing feature of these sharks is their teeth. A great hammerhead has triangular teeth with serrated edges. Jose Castro (1983) noted, "All the other hammerheads lack the strongly serrated teeth and the pelvic fins with curved rear margins."

The largest great hammerhead taken in North Carolina was a thirteen-foot-ten-inch-long female. She was caught by Russell Coles off Cape Lookout back in July 1918. Coles (1919) noted that he observed the shark for two weeks before finally harpooning the elusive fish. He wrote, "It is probable that within the previous two weeks, this large shark had eaten from my nets more than 50 sharks of about 6 ft. in length, leaving only their heads gilled in the net, and, with at least half a dozen species to select from, it was always her own species who she selected."

Coles's record may have been eclipsed by Cecil Nelson of Morehead City. A renowned shark fisherman in his own right, Nelson killed over six thousand sharks in the vicinity of Bogue Inlet during the years he operated a shark fishery in the waters off Carteret County between 1937 and 1948. Jack Shanley interviewed Nelson in 1948 for an article he wrote detailing the shark fisherman's exploits and an upcoming stint of fishing for sharks in the Red Sea. Shanley (1948) noted that the most notable shark Nelson remembered catching "was an eighteen-foot great hammerhead that weighed about a ton." Unfortunately, there is no specific mention of the exact date this hammerhead was caught nor a photograph of this notable hammerhead; otherwise, he would be credited with landing the largest great hammerhead ever taken along the North Carolina coast. The largest great hammerhead ever landed in South Carolina was caught by Byron Bass in August 1989. The shark measured twelve feet, seven and a half inches long and weighed 588.3 pounds.

The favourite food item for great hammerheads appears to be its fellow sharks and rays. Numerous fishermen through the years have related finding stingray barbs lodged in the digestive tracts of great hammerheads, a testimony to the last dying blow administered by a doomed ray.

Sometimes, these fish will even eat their own fellow hammerhead sharks. In 1919, Coles examined the aforementioned thirteen-foot-ten-inch female great hammerhead. This female had eaten fifty juvenile great hammerheads from his net. She chose these victims despite the fact that sharks of other species were readily available.

Great hammerheads are regarded as potentially dangerous to humans and have been chronicled attacking people in other parts of the world. But despite being found in in such large numbers off North Carolina, the hammerhead attack on Hall while surfing near the Emerald Isle Pier in 1976 remains the only documented hammerhead attack from Calabash to Currituck.

OCTOBER 1989
NEW HANOVER COUNTY, SPECIES UNKNOWN

Doug Nunnally, a New Hanover County schoolteacher with over two decades of experience as a recreational diver, decided to head out to spend time exploring one of the wrecks off Carolina Beach on October 8, 1989. He did not tell any of his friends or family members exactly where he was going nor why he had decided to explore the wrecks by himself. Tragically, the popular vocational education teacher went missing and could not provide further enlightenment, as he would never again be seen alive.

Officials could only speculate about what transpired during his final moments, as his boat was found adrift in the Frying Pan Shoals on October 10 by crewmen from the U.S. Coast Guard. A few days later, two fishermen spotted his body floating near the surface of the water a few miles off Carolina Beach. Press reports (Feldman, 1989) noted, "Robert Thompson, associate chief medical examiner in Chapel Hill, said he could not tell how long Nunnally had been in the water before dying or what caused his death. However, he said it appeared the 49-year-old had been attacked by a shark at some point."

Dr. Schwartz (2003) did not include Nunnally's attack in his list of shark fatalities from the Carolinas. However, he did state that he had seen photographs of the remains and was certain this was the handiwork of a large shark, most likely a tiger shark instead of a great white.

There is no way of knowing exactly which species of shark was responsible for this attack. The waters off Carolina Beach can be warm enough for bull sharks or tiger sharks to still be lurking about in early October.

May 1992
Carteret County, Sand Tiger Shark/
Carcharias taurus

In May 1992, Mike Weathers disappeared while scuba diving around the wreck of *U-352*, a German U-boat that was sunk during World War II approximately twenty miles off Beaufort Inlet. Weathers's dive seemed to be a routine one for him and his seven diving companions. But for reasons unknown, he turned around and headed back to the wreck. Had he dropped some valuable piece of gear? Was he confused? No one will ever know, as he never returned to the surface.

What most plausibly happened next is that he was killed by a shark, most likely one of the same sand tiger sharks that draw so many shark diving tourists to visit this particular wreck. Though his remains were not found, Brian Thomason of Newport found some damaged scuba gear near the wreck site a few days later, which was turned over to the coast guard. The gear, which had evidence of having been torn and chewed by a sand tiger shark, matched descriptions of what Weathers was carrying when he was last seen alive (Smith, 1992).

Mundus and Wisner (1971) noted that sand tiger sharks are well known for their voracious appetites.

Sand tigers are famous (or infamous if you happen to be a commercial fisherman) for their insatiable appetites. If other sharks are hungry 24 hours a day, these gluttons are voracious 48 hours a day. The stomachs of

A sand tiger shark as seen from below.

large sand tigers have contained as much as 100 pounds of food. Crabs,
squid and, occasionally, young lobsters have been found in their bellies at
Woods Hole Oceanographic Institute in Massachusetts. But mainly, they
feed upon smaller fishes, and the menu is almost as long as your arm....
According to observers who have seen them in feeding action, sand tigers will
attack a school of lesser fishes much as a wolf pack besets a deer or moose.
The species is notorious for its habit of raiding pound nets.

They are also considered to be much less dangerous to humans than tiger sharks, at least off the coast of North Carolina. Many tourists come each year to dive with sand tiger sharks off such wrecks as that of the tanker *Papoose*, which was sunk off Cape Lookout by a German U-boat in World War II. In Australia and South Africa, where these sharks are commonly known as grey nurse sharks and ragged tooth sharks, they have a more fearsome reputation.

However, sand tiger sharks are not completely harmless in the waters off North Carolina, as Weathers's death demonstrates. A *Carcharias taurus* was named as the culprit in an attack on a teenage girl who was swimming in waist-deep water off Shell Island Resort when she was bitten on the hand on July 17, 2010.

The ocean floor off the coast of North Carolina is littered with the remains of literally thousands of ships that have gone down in these waters. Many of these wreck sites have been popular targets for divers since the development of recreational scuba diving gear became widely available in the middle of the twentieth century. One thing that divers have observed is that these wreck sites are frequently visited by large numbers of sand tiger sharks. In October 1983, diver Roderick Farb discovered a shipwreck in the Atlantic Ocean off Ocracoke, North Carolina, which proved to be the elusive wreck of the submarine USS *Tarpon*. A study on this and subsequent dives showed that the wreck is frequented by large numbers of sand tiger sharks.

Farb (1998) noted:

> *Males, prior to mating, bite the female behind her head and forward of the first dorsal fin. In the process, the male shark loses some of his protruding teeth, and these fall to the bottom. Ordinarily, teeth lost during mating would go unnoticed on the bottom unless they fell on a substratum that would prevent them from being covered by sand. The Tarpon's hull provides this substratum. I have surveyed other shipwrecks that are a few miles*

Sand tiger sharks are frequently encountered by divers off the North Carolina coast.

further offshore of the submarine. Not only are there many sand tiger sharks present on these other sites, but the wreck hulls and adjacent bottom are also littered with their teeth.

As time passed, more sand tiger sharks were found at other dive sites in the area. Scientists now realize that the warm waters south of Cape Hatteras and west of the Gulf Stream down to Cape Lookout are frequented by sand tiger sharks for breeding purposes. The numerous sharks' teeth, which divers like Farb found on the wrecks on the ocean's bottom in this area, attest to the often violent behaviour meted out between sand tiger sharks while frequenting the waters off the southern Outer Banks.

Sand tiger sharks are frequently seen in aquariums around the world. This is because they have proven to be hardy and can adapt to living in captivity. Many species of sharks, such as the great white, will die in short order if kept in an aquarium. But sand tiger sharks rarely fail to adapt if given the proper care and fed adequately. Most aquariums feed their sharks on a regular schedule and supplement their diets with vitamins. All North Carolina aquariums have exhibits featuring live sand tiger sharks.

AUGUST 1993
CARTERET COUNTY, BULL SHARK / *CARCHARHINUS LEUCAS*

On August 15, 1993, Petra Rijdes was attacked while being towed behind her family's thirty-five-foot-long sailboat in the waters of Pamlico Sound near Brandt Island Shoal in Carteret County. After examining the wounds inflicted to the girl's abdomen and legs, Dr. Schwartz concluded that the shark responsible for the attack was a bull shark measuring approximately seven feet long.

1999
NEW HANOVER COUNTY, BASKING SHARK / *CETORHINUS MAXIMUS*

The second-largest species of shark that inhabits the waters of coastal North Carolina is the basking shark, *Cetorhinus maximus*. These sharks sometimes attain a size as long as forty-nine and a half feet, but they rarely grow more than thirty-three feet in length. The basking shark is second in size only to the whale shark and thus has the distinction of being the second-largest fish in the world. Basking sharks, fortunately, are fairly docile creatures. Despite their apparent harmless disposition, however, they sometimes pose a threat to those who get too close. For instance, in the winter of 1999, a thirty-eight-foot-long fishing boat sank after colliding with one of these large sharks in the waters near the Frying Pan Shoals.

The boat was the *Bird Dog*, a sportfishing boat that operated out of Carolina Beach. Its captain, Buddy Severt, and two crew members were cruising on calm waters about eighteen miles southeast of Cape Fear when they inadvertently ran up on a basking shark floating along on the surface of the sea, apparently feeding. In the collision, the boat lost its running gear and had a big hole ripped out of its hull. The damage done to the shark is unknown.

The sea raced in through the opening in the hull, quickly filling *Bird Dog* with water and causing it to sink. Fortunately, Severt and the crew were able to make a quick escape in an inflatable raft. A distress call was made before abandoning ship, and a nearby fishing boat, the *Mike A Bee*, picked up Severt and his men. They were later transferred to another fishing boat, the *Class Action*, which was bound for Carolina Beach. Fortunately, all hands were safe, despite their encounter with the second-largest fish species in the ocean.

The *Bird Dog* has the distinction of being the only vessel in the North Carolina known to have been sunk by a shark. It is a wonder more vessels did not suffer the same fate as the *Bird Dog*, as the seas around the Frying Pan Shoals were filled with basking sharks. Dr. Schwartz later received reports of a school consisting of one hundred of these enormous fish that was observed on February 11, 1999, in the vicinity of Frying Pan and Cape Fear.

A basking shark caught off Salter Path in April 1947. The shark is shown in front of Ottis' Fish Market in Morehead City. *Photograph courtesy of North Carolina Archives and History.*

In the North Atlantic, basking sharks prefer the cool waters of more northerly climes, but in the winter, they migrate south to feed on plankton blooms. They are found in the coastal waters of the Carolinas during the winter months, usually in late winter, as they work their way back toward the north to their preferred home in the cooler waters off the coasts of places like Newfoundland, Iceland and Great Britain.

As they cruise along the North Carolina coast, basking sharks can often be seen feeding just offshore beyond the breakers. A basking shark feeds by opening its mouth and allowing large amounts of water to pass through its gills, where plankton and crustaceans are filtered out in its gill arches, much in the same way a baleen whale feeds.

One of the earliest mentions of a basking shark off the East Coast of the United States was about a shark caught near Charleston in November 1826 by Newman Kershaw and two unidentified individuals. A press account (anonymous, 1826) stated that the shark was twelve feet long, two feet across the back "and weighed 400 pounds." Another early account of a basking shark from the Carolinas was penned by Russell Coles (1915). Coles nearly harpooned one off Cape Lookout in July 1905. Though he got within twenty yards of his prey, in this case, the "big one" got away.

The first recorded taking of a basking shark along the North Carolina coast occurred in February 1935. A thirteen-foot-five-inch-long female was captured in a shad net near Corncake Inlet, just offshore from Bald Head Island. The shark was quickly put into the hands of H.H. Brimley of the State Museum in Raleigh, who studied it in detail, hoping to later reproduce a model of the fish for his collection. He pointed out that prior to this basking shark, the most southerly occurrence of this species documented in the scientific literature from a locale along the shores of the United States was in Sea Girt, New Jersey.

Brimley (1935) described the teeth and gills of this rare shark. "The teeth are numerous, recurved, and very small, with no cutting edges, the exposed part of the longest tooth being only about one sixteenth of an inch in length. The gill-rakers are highly developed and are used much as are the whalebone plates in the baleen whales, for straining from the water that flows into the mouth the small forms of marine life on which the animal feeds."

These sharks share another trait often associated with whales. On numerous occasions, basking sharks have beached themselves on the North Carolina coast. For instance, in March 2000, two basking sharks, measuring twenty-five feet and twenty-eight feet, respectively, beached themselves within a twenty-four period on North Topsail Beach. Sometimes, large

Bull shark sightings have been reported in the waters of Albemarle Sound off Edenton.

schools of these fish beach themselves, as happened along the coast from Cape Hatteras to the Bogue Banks in 1987 and 1988.

During the twentieth century, several basking sharks were sighted along the coast of the Carolinas. In North Carolina alone, Schwartz (2002) counted 364 basking sharks from 1901 through 2002. "Fishermen and the public accounted for 151 live sightings, while 183 stranded basking sharks were measured between 1970 and 2000."

In the spring of 1947, two basking sharks were caught by two different fishermen on the same day, April 25, off the Bogue Banks. The first was taken near a place known as the Hoop Hole Woods by Captain Leo Gillikin of Morehead City. This shark, which measured thirteen feet, six inches long, was hauled into Morehead City and hoisted up for the curious onlookers to see. The second basking shark was captured by Captain Gordon Lewis, also of Morehead City. His shark was approximately thirteen feet long and was taken approximately two and a half miles away from the first basking shark. This basking shark was taken in forty feet of water two miles off Salter Path. Captain Lewis brought his catch back to town and put it on display at Ottis' Fish Market on the waterfront.

When writing a report about the two basking sharks that were taken off the Bogue Banks, E.W. Gudger (1948) observed that sharks of this species had been known to travel in small groups. "Being gregarious in its habits, it is said to loaf often in the sunshine in small companies. Several writers have noted that two or three will sometimes swim in tandem fashion with their dorsal fins high out of the water—each observed occurrence possibly giving rise to another sea serpent story."

9

SOME EARLY TWENTY-FIRST-CENTURY

SHARK ATTACKS

The main purpose of writing this book is to chronicle some of the early shark attacks that are often overlooked by researchers. Today, organizations like the International Shark Attack File stand ready to document the minutest details of shark attacks on people anywhere in the world. However, I would be remiss to pass over some of the more notable recent fatal attacks that have occurred in North Carolina waters.

SEPTEMBER 2001
DARE COUNTY, TIGER SHARK/*GALEOCERDO CUVIER*

In 2001, the attention of the nation was focused on a series of particularly brutal shark attacks off Virginia and the Outer Banks of North Carolina. On September 3, 2001, a young Russian couple was wading in waist-deep the waters off Avon when they were attacked by what is believed to have been a tiger shark. The man, Sergei Zaloukaev, died of his wounds. His fiancée, Natalia Slobodskaya, lost her foot to the shark but survived the ordeal (anonymous, 2001).

This particular shark attack drew considerable media attention due to the fact that it was one of two fatal shark attacks that occurred over the Labour Day weekend. On September 1, 2001, ten-year-old David Peltier was mortally wounded by a bull shark while swimming with his family at

Bull shark sightings have been reported in the Chowan River.

Virginia Beach, Virginia. Two days later and 130 miles down the coast, Zaloukaev and Slobodskaya were attacked in Avon.

The media frenzy came to an abrupt halt as the nation's attention shifted north with the terrorist attacks on the Pentagon and World Trade Center on September 11, 2001.

SEPTEMBER 2009

CURRITUCK COUNTY, TIGER SHARK/*GALEOCERDO CUVIER*

At 10:00 p.m. on September 12, 2009, Richard Snead went for a swim in the ocean by his hotel in Corolla. He and his wife had just arrived at the beach after a trip from their home in Pittsburgh, Pennsylvania. Tragically, he was never seen alive again. Investigators from the Currituck County Sheriff's Department found his glasses lying on his towel on the beach near Mile Post 5 and deduced that the sixty-year-old went for a late-night swim. Searchers from both Currituck County as well as U.S. Coast Guard personnel combed the beaches of the area and conducted sweeps of the waters offshore but gave up hope of perhaps finding him still alive and called off the search. His remains were found five days after he originally went for his swim approximately twenty miles to the south at Kill Devil Hills.

Medical examiners from Greenville originally reported that Snead had died as the result of blood loss due to a shark attack. However, an outside group was hired by local business and tourism promoters to take another look, and they concluded that Snead had, in their opinion, actually drowned an instant before bleeding to death from his grievous shark bite, thus making his official cause of death drowning instead of being the result of a shark bite. This may seem, at first glance, an odd way of splitting hairs over the poor man's final milliseconds, but it goes to show the great lengths promoters continue to go downplaying such incidents.

Based on an examination of the bite marks, investigators determined that the attack was made by a *Galeocerdo cuvier*. There was also evidence that other animals had been feeding on the remains as they drifted down the beach, but the initial strike was made by a tiger shark.

10

ANALYZING THE DATA

ariners cast a wary eye at the North Carolina coast for good reason—not just because of the treacherous storms and violent weather but also because of perils waiting underneath the surface of the sea should they have the misfortune of being plunged into the waters of the Graveyard of the Atlantic. Fatal shark attacks have occurred off North Carolina for more than two centuries. As humans continue to flock to the coast, attacks will no doubt continue to happen.

Sharks have long been one of the natural hazards faced by people along the North Carolina coast. The exact number of shark attacks that have

Thresher shark.

occurred along the state's coast over the past five centuries will never be known; though if we include both nearshore and offshore waters, one can estimate that it must be in the thousands. Many victims, especially during the eighteenth and nineteenth centuries, seldom returned to report their own personal misadventure.

Despite millions of dollars being spent by governments across the globe, no one has yet figured out exactly why some sharks are compelled to attack people. Every type of shark attack researchers have identified in studies conducted for civilian and military purposes—both provoked and unprovoked—have occurred in Tar Heel waters. As populations of large, aggressive sharks, such as tiger sharks, great whites and bull sharks, continue to rebound thanks to the success of global conservation efforts that were started in the late twentieth century, lethal encounters between these apex predators will continue in the "shark-haunted waters" off North Carolina.

SOME SHARKS FOUND
OFF THE COAST OF NORTH CAROLINA

The following is a list of several shark species found off the coast of North Carolina.

Atlantic angel shark	*Squatina dumeril*
Atlantic sharpnose shark	*Rhizoprionodon terrenovae*
basking shark	*Cetorhinus maximus*
bigeye thrasher shark	*Alopias superciliosus*
bignose shark	*Carcharhinus altimus*
black dogfish	*Deania profundorum*
blacknose shark	*Carcharhinus acronotus*
blacktip shark	*Carcharhinus limbatus*
Blainville's dogfish	*Squalus blainvillei*
blue shark	*Prionace glauca*
bonnethead	*Sphyrna tiburo*
bramble shark	*Echinorhinus brucus*
bull shark	*Carcharhinus leucas*
Carolina hammerhead	*Sphyrna gilgerti*
chain dogfish	*Scyliorhinus retifer*
cookie-cutter shark	*Isistius brasiliensis*
Cuban dogfish	*Squalus cubensis*
dusky shark	*Carcharhinus obscurus*
finetooth shark	*Apionodon isodon*
Galapagos shark	*Carcharhinus galapagensis*

great hammerhead	*Sphyrna mokarran*
great white shark	*Carcharodon carcharias*
Greenland shark	*Somniosus microcephalus*
lemon shark	*Negaprion brevirostris*
marbled cat shark	*Galeus arae*
night shark	*Hypoprion signatus*
nurse shark	*Ginglymostoma cirratum*
oceanic whitetip shark	*Carcharhinus longimanus*
porbeagle shark	*Lamna nasus*
sandbar shark	*Carcharhinus milberti*
sand tiger shark	*Odontaspis taurus*
scalloped hammerhead	*Sphyrna lewini*
shortfin mako shark	*Isurus oxyrinchus*
silky shark	*Carcharhinus falciformis*
sixgill shark	*Hexanchus griseus*
smooth dogfish	*Mustelus canis*
smooth hammerhead	*Sphyrna zygaena*
spinner shark	*Carcharhinus maculipinnis*
spiny dogfish	*Squalus acanthias*
thresher shark	*Alopias vulpinus*
tiger shark	*Galeocerdo cuvieri*
whale shark	*Rhincodon typus*

TOP TEN SPECIES FOR UNPROVOKED SHARK ATTACKS FROM 1580 TO 2022

	Species	Number of Unprovoked Attacks
1. great white shark	*Carcharodon carcharias*	354
2. tiger shark	*Galeocerdo cuvier*	138
3. bull shark	*Carcharhinus leucas*	131
4. requiem shark	*Carcharinus spp.*	69
5. blacktip shark	*Carcharhinus limbatus*	41
6. sand tiger shark	*Carcharias taurus*	36
7. wobbegong shark	*Orectolobus spp.*	19
8. hammerhead shark	*Sphyrna spp.*	16
8. spinner shark	*Carcharhinus brevipinna*	16
10. bronze whaler shark	*Carcharhinus brachyurus*	15

BIBLIOGRAPHY

Albany Evening Post. "Rescue of Nine More of the Crew of the *William Penn.*" October 13, 1855.

Alexandria Gazette. October 11, 1864.

Allen, Thomas B. *Shadows in the Sea, the Sharks, Skates and Rays.* Philadelphia: Chilton Books, 1963.

Arthur, Billy. "Down East." *Onslow County New and View,* March 27, 1945.

Baum, Julia K., et al. "Collapse and Conservation of Shark Populations in the Northwest Atlantic." *Science* 299 (2003): 389–92.

Beaufort Weekly Record. "A Monster Shark." May 18, 1888.

Bell, J.C., and J.T. Nichols. "Notes on the Food of Carolina Sharks." *Copeia* 22 (1921): 17–20.

Bigelow, Henry B., and William C. Schroeder. "Fishes of the Gulf of Maine." *Fishery Bulletin of the Fish and Wildlife Service* 53 (1953).

———. *Fishes of the Western North Atlantic.* Part 1. *Sharks.* New Haven, CT: Memoir Sears Foundation for Marine Research Number I, 1948.

Bowers, Matthew. "Case of Swimmer Thought Killed by Shark Reviewed." *Virginian-Pilot,* October 17, 2009.

Bright, Michael. *The Private Life of Sharks.* Mechanicsburg, PA: Stackpole Books, 2000.

Brimley, H.H. "Basking Shark (Cetorhinus Maximus) in North Carolina Waters." *Journal of the Elisha Mitchell Scientific Society* 51 (1935): 311.

———. "Notes on the Occurrence of a Whale Shark (Rhincodon Typus) in the Cape Fear River, Near Southport, N.C." *Journal of the Elisha Mitchell Scientific Society* 51 (1935): 160–62.

Brown, Aycock. "Maneaters Rare Off Coast." *News and Observer*, May 28, 1950.

Burton, E. Milby. "A Record Tiger Shark from South Carolina." *Copeia* 1 (1941): 40.

———. "Shark Attacks along the South Carolina Coast." *Scientific Monthly* 40 (1935): 279–83.

Carolina Watchman. "Eaten by a Shark." June 22, 1876.

Casey, J.G., and N.E. Kohler. "Long Distance Movements of Atlantic Sharks from the NMFS Cooperative Shark Tagging Program." *Discovering Sharks*, 1990.

Castro, Jose. "The Shark Nursery of Bulls Bay, South Carolina, with a View of the Shark Nurseries of the Southeastern United States." *Environmental Biology of Fishes* 38 (1993): 37–48.

———. *The Sharks of North America*. Oxford, UK: Oxford University Press, 2011.

———. *The Sharks of North American Waters*. College Station: Texas A&M University Press, 1983.

Charleston Courier. "At Smithville, NC." July 16, 1812.

Charlotte Democrat. "North Carolina News Items." April 23, 1875.

———. "North Carolina News Items." July 22, 1882.

Charlotte Observer. "Shark Attacks Atlantic Man." June 30, 1916.

Clayton, Cindy, and Patrick Wilson. "Autopsy: Shark Killed Man Who Washed Up in Kill Devil Hills." *Virginian Pilot*, September 19, 2009.

Coles, Russell J. "The Large Sharks of Cape Lookout, North Carolina: The White Shark or Maneater, Tiger Shark and Hammerhead." *Copeia* 69 (1919): 34–35.

———. "Notes on the Sharks and Rays of Cape Lookout, N.C." *Proceedings of the Biological Society of Washington* 28 (1915): 89–94.

Dallas Morning News. "Water Infested with Sharks." November 15, 1937.

Dawson, William. "Note on a Shark and Ray Obtained at Little Metis, on the Lower St. Lawrence." *Canadian Record of Science* (April 1891): 303–9.

Detroit Free Press. "Navy Reveals Sinking of Cuban Freighter." December 10, 1943.

Duncan, Thomas. "Drowned by a Shark." *Charleston News and Courier*, July 30, 1905.

Dunn, Andrew. "Doctor: Sand Tiger Shark Likely Culprit for 13-Year-Old Bitten Near Shell Island Resort." *Wilmington Star News*, July 17, 2010.

Farb, Roderick. *Shipwrecks Diving the Graveyard of the Atlantic*. 2nd ed. Birmingham, AL: Menasha Ridge Press, 1998.

Farmer & Mechanic. "A Chapter of Accidents." July 10, 1879.

Feldman, Alison. "Expert Identifies Body as Nunnally." *Wilmington Morning Star*, October 17, 1989.

Fox, A. Lane. "Primitive Warfare: Illustrated by Specimens from the Museum of the Institution." *Journal of the Royal United Service Institution* 11 (1868): 612–45.

Gilbert, Perry W., ed. *Sharks and Survival*. Boston: D.C. Heath & Company, 1963.

Goerch, Carl. "Diamond Lightship Sits Astride Gulf Stream and Warns Ships Against Treacherous Shoals." *Greensboro Daily News*, August 25, 1957.

"Greek Freighter Sinks off Cape Hatteras." *Life* 3, no. 22 (1937): 26.

Greensboro Daily News. "Cuban Seaman Is Treated for Shark Bite." December 13, 1943.

———. "Maneater Caught in River." June 14, 1941.

———. "Shark Chaser Bitten at State Beach." September 11, 1947.

———. "Shark Takes Chunk out of Youth's Leg." July 2, 1940.

Greensboro Record. "Baker Is Bitten by Denizen of the Deep." May 27, 1936.

———. "Two 13-Year-Old Youths Battle Maddened Sharks." August 25, 1936.

Gudger, E.W. "The Basking Shark, *Cetorhinus maximus*, on the North Carolina Coast." *Journal of the Elisha Mitchell Scientific Society* 64 (1948): 41–44.

———. "Sizes Attained by the Large Hammerhead Sharks." *Copeia* 4 (1947): 228–36.

———. "The Tiger Shark, *Galeocerdo tigrinus*, on the North Carolina Coast and Its Feeding Habits There." *Journal of the Elisha Mitchell Scientific Society* 64 (1948): 221–33.

Halstead, Bruce W. *Dangerous Marine Animals*. Cambridge, MA: Cornell Maritime Press, 1959.

Haskin, Frederick J. "Skinning the Shark." *Wyoming State Tribune*, June 24, 1918.

Hendersonville Times-News. "Shark Didn't Attack." August 30, 1976.

Henry, Michael. "25-Foot Shark Snared by Net, Dies." *Outer Banks Sentinel*, March 23, 2002.

Herdendorf, Charles E., and Tim M. Berra. "A Greenland Shark from the Wreck of the SS *Central America* at 2,200 Meters." *Transactions of the American Fisheries Society* 124, no. 6 (1995): 950–53.

Heyer, Patricia, and Robert Heyer. *Shark Attacks of the Jersey Shore*. Charleston, SC: The History Press, 2020.

Holloman, William. "The Real Jaws." *State*, August 24–25, 1986.

Huish, Melvin T., and Christopher Benedict. "Sonic Tracking of Dusky Sharks in the Cape Fear River, North Carolina." *Journal of the Elisha Mitchell Scientific Society* 93, no. 1 (1977): 21–36.

Jenson, A.S. *The Selachians of Greenland*. Copenhagen, DK: Bianco Lunos Bogtrykkeri, 1914.

Lee, Morgan. "Basking Shark Sinks 'Bird Dog.'" *Wilmington Morning Star*, February 26, 1999.

Massmann, William H. "Shark Danger in Chesapeake Seen Slight." *Richmond Times-Dispatch*, October 14–16, 1953.

Mundus, Frank, and Bill Wisner. *Sportfishing for Sharks*. New York: MacMillan Company, 1971.

Musick, Jack. "Details of the Attacks, September 1–3, 2001." *Report of the Virginia Shark Attack Task Force*, 2001.

New Bern Journal. "Funeral for Shark Victim." September 22, 1935.

News and Observer. "Dragged Down by Tiger of the Sea." July 30, 1905.

New York Times. "Sharks Swallow Sailor." May 8, 1939.

Nielsen, Julius, et. al. "Eye Lens Radiocarbon Reveals Centuries of Longevity in the Greenland Shark (*Somniosus microcephalus*)." *Science* 353, no. 6,300 (2016): 702–4.

Olds, Fred A. "Echoes of Pioneer Days." *Charlotte Observer*, February 11, 1906.

Quatro, Jospeh M., William B. Driggers III, James M. Grady, Glenn F. Ulrich and Mark A. Roberts. "Sphyrna Gilbert Sp. Nov., a New Hammerhead Shark (*Carcharhiniformes sphyrnidae*) from the Western Atlantic Ocean." *Zootaxa* 3,702, no. 2 (2008): 159–78.

Radcliffe, Lewis. "The Sharks and Rays of Beaufort, North Carolina." *Bulletin of the U.S. Bureau of Fisheries* 34 (1914): 239–384.

Reaves, Bill. "Sharks of North Carolina." Unpublished manuscript, Bill Reaves Collection, New Hanover County Public Library, 2000.

Richmond Times Dispatch. "Grim Fight for Life Related by Survivors." November 16, 1937.

Rockford Register. "Shark Fatality First in NC Since 1957." September 5, 2001.

Sawyer, Francine. "Once Endangered Shark May Be Making Comeback." *Jacksonville Daily News*, March 16, 2000.

Scharp, Hal. *Shark Safari*. New York: A.S. Barnes & Company, 1975.

Schwartz, Frank. "Basking and Whale Sharks of North Carolina." *Journal of the North Carolina Academy of Science* 126, no. 3 (2010): 84–87.

———. "Basking Sharks, *Cetorhinus maximus*, Family Cetorhinidae, Recorded in North Carolina Waters 1901–2002." *Journal of the North Carolina Academy of Science* 118, no. 3 (2002): 202–2.

———. "Bull Sharks of North Carolina." *Journal of the North Carolina Academy of Science* 128, no. 3 (2012): 88–91.

———. "Elasmobranchs of the Cape Fear River." *Journal of the Elisha Mitchell Scientific Society* 116, no. 3 (2000): 206–44.

———. "Food of Tiger Sharks, *Galeocerdo cuvier* (Carcharhinidae) from the Northwest Atlantic Ocean, off North Carolina." *Journal of the Elisha Mitchell Scientific Society* 116, no. 4 (2000): 351–55.

———. *Sharks, Sawfish, Skates and Rays of the Carolinas*. Morehead City: UNC Institute of Marine Sciences, 1989.

———. *Sharks, Skates and Rays of the Carolinas*. Chapel Hill: UNC Press, 2003.

Schwartz, Frank, and George H. Burgess. *Sharks of North Carolina and Adjacent Waters*. Raleigh: North Carolina Department of Natural and Economic Resources, Division of Marine Fisheries, 1975.

Shanley, Jack. "Shark Fisherman to Angle Abroad." *New York Times*, April 6, 1948.

Shaw, Francis Fountain, and Annie Fountain. "The Tragic Death of Jere Wilson Fountain." In *The John R. Fountain Family of Onslow County, North Carolina*. N.p.: privately published, 1992.

Smith, Hugh M. "The Fishes of North Carolina." *Bulletin of the North Carolina Geological and Economic Survey*, 1907.

Smith, Richard F. "Chewed Scuba Gear Found Near Where Diver Disappeared." *Wilmington Morning Star*, June 19, 1992.

Springfield Republican. "A Diver's Adventure with a Shark." February 4, 1884.

Stillwell, Chuck. "The Ravenous Mako." *Underwater Naturalist, Bulletin of the American Littoral Society*, special double issue, 19, no. 4; 20, no. 1 (1990): 77–78.

Tarboro Press. "A Strange Adventure." September 21, 1839.

Trenton Evening Examiner. "Shark Kills Swimmer." July 16, 1957.

Troy Record. "Seamen Saved from Submarine and Sharks." December 13, 1943.

Warren Ledger. "Newbern." June 15, 1894.

Weekly Commercial. "Supposed Shipwreck." October 4, 1849.

W.G.T. "A Sad Tragedy at Beaufort." *News and Observer*, July 7, 1879.

Whiteaves, J.F. *Catalogue of Canadian Pinnipedia, Cetacea, Fishes and Marine Invertebrata*. Ottawa, CA: Department of Fisheries of the Dominion of Canada, Canadian Department of Fisheries, 1886.

Wilmington Daily Journal. "Bitten by a Shark." July 31, 1870.
Wilmington News. "Shark Caught Near Masonboro." April 9, 1948.
Wilmington Star. "Elizabeth City." September 9, 1881.

ABOUT THE AUTHOR

John Hairr is an award-winning writer and geo-historian who explores the world investigating the planet's natural wonders and historical mysteries. He has written extensively about the natural history of the southeastern United States, especially his home state of North Carolina, with works covering a wide range of maritime topics such as sharks, shipwrecks and extinct wildlife.

Visit us at
www.historypress.com